LINKEDIN FOR STUDENTS, GRADUATES, AND EDUCATORS

Copyright © Melonie Dodaro, Miguel Ángel Garcia Elizondo 2019.
All Rights Reserved.

Edited by: Ahna Weisser
No part of this publication may be reproduced, stored in a retrieval system, or transmitted in any form or by any means, electronic, mechanical, photocopy, recording, or otherwise, without prior written permission of the copyright owner. Nor can it be circulated in any form of binding or cover other than that in which it is published and without similar condition including this condition being imposed on a subsequent purchaser. Any queries relating to this publication or author may be sent to info@topdogsocialmedia.com

ISBN-13: 9781698414294

This book is in no way authorized by, endorsed by, or affiliated with LinkedIn or its subsidiaries. All references to LinkedIn and other trademarked properties are used in accordance with the Fair Use Doctrine and are not meant to imply that this book is a LinkedIn product for advertising or other commercial purposes.

Bulk discounts may be available for university training programs. For details, email: info@topdogsocialmedia.com

This book is available in print and electronic formats. Please visit **LinkedInForStudentsBook.com** for details.

LINKEDIN FOR STUDENTS, GRADUATES, AND EDUCATORS

HOW TO USE LINKEDIN TO LAND YOUR DREAM JOB IN 90 DAYS: A CAREER DEVELOPMENT HANDBOOK

MELONIE DODARO
MIGUEL ÁNGEL GARCIA ELIZONDO

Copyright © Melonie Dodaro, Miguel Ángel Garcia Elizondo 2019.
All Rights Reserved.

CONTENTS

Preface vii
Introduction. ix
Part I: Laying Your Career Foundation 1
Chapter 1: What Is LinkedIn and Why Use It? 3
Chapter 2: Defining Who You Are and Whom You Want to Become. 19
Chapter 3: Turning Students into Sought-After Professionals 29
Chapter 4: LinkedIn Etiquette and Best Practices. 39
Chapter 5: Determine Your Target Audience and Ideal Employers 49
Part II: Your Path to Career Development on LinkedIn **59**
Chapter 6: Design Your LinkedIn Profile 61
Chapter 7: Build Relationships and Open Doors 75
Chapter 8: Effective Messaging Tactics to Connect with Decision-Makers . . . 89
Chapter 9: Engage with Your Network to Stand Out from the Crowd 99
Chapter 10: Moving from Content Curator to Content Creator 107
Part III: Applying LinkedIn Beyond the Basics. **121**
Chapter 11: LinkedIn Action Steps for Your Career Planning. 123
Chapter 12: LinkedIn for Educators: Prepare Students for Success 157
Conclusion. 171
About the Authors 173
References 175

PREFACE

What if I told you there was a tool that could help you establish your career before you left university? Or that once you graduate, this tool could be the ultimate difference between finding an okay job that pays your bills and building a meaningful career that makes your dreams possible?

Students and graduates had had access to this tool since before Facebook, Twitter, and YouTube even existed, but it's one of the least used and most misunderstood of all the major social media platforms by this demographic.

That statistic isn't surprising. To use a tool effectively, you need to know what it is, how it works, why it works, and what success looks like when you apply it to different challenges and opportunities.

Here are Miguel's reflections on his journey with LinkedIn.com:

"I can't remember the exact day I joined, but one thing certainly stands out. As a first-time intern and university student logging into LinkedIn, I didn't feel I fit in. It felt as if I showed up at a business conference with people who looked much older, wiser, and more interesting than me. That begged the question: if I didn't feel I belonged on LinkedIn, why should I bother showing up again? It would be several years before I logged back into the platform.

Unlike other social media platforms, where I connected with friends, watched funny videos, or followed my favorite artists, LinkedIn did not appeal much or make sense to me as an undergraduate student. It was only after several years (and many lessons) that I realized how little I understood about the professional value of social media and what I needed to do to succeed with LinkedIn. This is what I want to help you avoid and achieve—earlier rather than later. You'll see the difference not only in your earning potential but, more importantly, in the level of fulfillment you'll have in your work."

See whether this book belongs in your hands or in the hands of someone you care about. The following is a list of people we believe will benefit the most from our book:

- undergraduate students
- postgraduate students
- part-time students
- graduates
- interns, apprentices, or those seeking mentors and work experience
- educators
- career development and career services professionals
- parents or any family members who care about education

The purpose of this book is to help students, graduates, and educators learn how to use LinkedIn as part of their career development plans. Within these pages, we share our knowledge, experience, exercises, activities, best practices, relevant stories, and tools that can be applied easily, practically, and immediately to make any job search a success.

This book is a series of small steps and actions you can take as you read each page and finish each chapter. The results will change the way you see yourself and manage your future, preparing you for your ideal career.

We hope you'll join us on this journey.

Are you ready?

Melonie Dodaro and Miguel Ángel Garcia Elizondo

INTRODUCTION

My name is Miguel Ángel Garcia Elizondo, and I could tell you many things to establish my expertise and credibility on everything you're about to read. Instead, I'll share a short story that highlights my passion for what I do.

This book would not be possible without LinkedIn. You see, when I started working at LinkedIn in 2015, I did something that transformed my life and career. However, at the time, I didn't realize the extent of the change. After spending my first few months on the job, coaching my customers on ways to engage with their networks to sell more effectively, I decided it was time to walk the talk. To build my credibility, I was going to use LinkedIn to develop my own brand and connect with the top social-selling influencers across the world.

After researching a variety of different sources, articles, and posts on social media, I came across an interesting report listing the top 25 social selling influencers. These included TED speakers, bestselling authors, and very successful entrepreneurs. Although I felt there was a very slim chance any of them would connect with me and reply on LinkedIn, I decided to give it a shot. I put together short messages, telling my prospects how I found them and what I wanted to achieve and offered my help with anything if they ever visited London. Then I pressed the "Send" button, hoping to get at least one reply.

Within a few hours, I was reading the first reply. A week later, most of these influencers had connected with me and replied to me on LinkedIn. Luckily, one of those individuals was Melonie Dodaro, bestselling author of

LinkedIn Unlocked and *The LinkedIn Code*. Melonie told me she would be visiting London in the following few weeks and needed help finding a small venue for a meetup she was hosting. I gave her pub recommendations and came to her meetup myself, finally meeting her in person.

A couple of years later, Melonie and I started discussing how we could share our LinkedIn expertise with students. That's when we began writing this book for you!

None of this would have happened without us following our own advice and employing the best LinkedIn practices we are about to share with you. It's why we believe in this book and why we know it can help you, too. I hope this book can be the spark to imagine, find, and do work that means something important to you *and* the world.

Looking back, I can't believe it took me just ten minutes to write a message that changed my life and career. What will be *your* story of success?

We wrote this book because we believe that putting students in control of their education and careers is among the most important things we can do for them. LinkedIn is a tool that's brought us tremendous success. In our journey to help companies and professionals, we've realized that students, university educators, and graduates can also benefit enormously from the opportunities this tool offers. We understand that LinkedIn doesn't cater to students and that the effort involved in using it effectively can seem daunting, but neither of these excuses is good enough for us. The new opportunities and ways of working can't be ignored.

Using our combined experience working with professionals, educators, and students, we've divided this book into three parts. We structured the flow of information to make it easy for you to understand and implement the lessons from this book.

Part one, the foundation of the book, explains why LinkedIn can be such a transformative tool for students and graduates. We describe what it is and how you'll be using it. Next, we help you define yourself and whom you wish to become a few years from now. These goals will be crucial when it comes to searching and applying for jobs as well as preparing for and attending interviews. Understanding and managing yourself are the first steps in finding a career that matters to you. You'll read stories about other students who went from not having a LinkedIn profile to getting multiple job offers within a few months of creating one.

Next, we discuss ways for students to become professionals during their school years, not after. This may seem like a significant mindset shift, but it's a necessary one as we consider the changing world of work. Your university path should be seen as not only a student journey but also a professional one. We discuss the essential skills and experience employers expect you to have from day one in nearly every field of work and show you how you can use LinkedIn to help you fill in some of the gaps left by your studies. This chapter will help you start thinking like the people and companies looking for the best candidates.

Further, we dive into LinkedIn etiquette and best practices so you can use it like a pro from the get go. Here, we look at your current online presence and the way LinkedIn differs from other social media channels. Even if you use social media every day, it will still be vital for you to know the difference between your activities on LinkedIn and other social platforms. We end part one by helping you determine your target audience and ideal employers so that you're spending your time only on the most valuable activities on LinkedIn. All this will lead you to find the right companies and jobs that align with who you are and whom you want to become.

Part two helps you move from planning to building. Going way beyond the information on your resume, you'll start creating a LinkedIn profile that attracts the right people and companies. We help you set up your profile with the essentials you need to have from day one and show you how you can earn an all-star profile. You'll learn what makes a great LinkedIn profile in your industry by looking at the best relevant profile examples so you can do better!

Once you feel proud of your profile, you'll start building relationships that open doors. We show you how to search for and find the right people and decision-makers across LinkedIn. By using your existing university and alumni networks, you'll learn how to quickly connect with people who may be able to offer you premium information or warm introductions that'll make all the difference in your job search. You'll understand what to look for in their profiles and how to use what you find to make them your allies.

The next steps will teach you how to use your new knowledge to connect with and message key influencers and decision-makers. We show you how to approach people beyond those you know on LinkedIn. You'll learn ways to put together connection requests that get accepted and messages that get replies. We share a range of different messaging tactics and templates so you can write your own. Whatever the outcome of your efforts is, you'll always be able to respond and pivot appropriately by employing the best practices shared in this book. You're in for a confidence boost!

As you get comfortable building relationships, the next chapters will show you how to engage effectively with your whole network and stand out from the crowd. Here, we show examples of what profitable engagement looks like and how you can share relevant content useful to your audience. These examples will help you curate engaging content, share unique perspectives, and spark valuable conversations that position you as much more than just a student or graduate looking for a job.

Your LinkedIn activity will have the potential to reach thousands of recruiters, hiring managers, and other employers looking for candidates who demonstrate their passion and expertise in their industries. Creating the right content exponentially increases your chances of being spotted by the right person, from the right company, with the right job offer. Does it get any better than that?

Yes, it does! For the most ambitious students and graduates, we've saved the last chapter in part two. In it, we discuss how you can move from being merely a content *curator* to a content *creator*. This means you write and publish your own content on LinkedIn instead of re-purposing and sharing the content of others. LinkedIn has its own publishing tool that millions of members use every day to share their ideas, thoughts, knowledge, and stories. Any posts you publish will appear on your profile, making it even easier for anyone who views it to spot your original work.

We'll help you find your voice as you explore possible topics you could write about and become comfortable sharing your work with your network. If you're still in school, you'll see how you can use some of your assignments and projects to showcase what you know and care about. We also cover the differences between academic and business writing. Sorry to say it, but not everything you learned in school will be useful on LinkedIn. But isn't that why you got this book?

If you've graduated, you'll still be able to find topics to write on that align with the career you're looking for. Nothing works better than telling your own story in the right way, in the right place, and at the right time. By the end of this chapter, you'll understand why publishing original content on LinkedIn will put you way ahead of the pack and supercharge your journey toward your ideal career.

Part three is dedicated to reviewing and applying everything you learned in the previous two parts. Our exercises will help you define your career sweet spot as well as your goals and ways of measuring your success throughout your LinkedIn journey. This is why we've chosen the highly effective 90-day framework as part of your overall strategy so you never have to spend too much time on any one step and can celebrate both the small and big wins. You'll also read stories of other undergraduate and postgraduate students who have gone through our workshops and have seen real results.

The final chapter of this book is written for educators. Professors, teaching assistants, social media/digital education professionals, and career services staff will benefit from reading this chapter.

If you are an educator, you'll learn how to make LinkedIn an essential part of the curriculum and inspire students to use it, getting value from it quickly. We share assessment templates you can use to measure your students' progress across a variety of areas on LinkedIn. We created this tool because we wanted to support you as you prepare your students for the jobs of today and tomorrow—not to mention the fact that you could quite possibly become the coolest, most helpful mentor on campus in the process.

In this final chapter, even high school educators can see how including LinkedIn in their lesson plans can be a huge confidence boost for their students. You'll read a story about a high school teacher who encouraged grade 11 students from his entrepreneurship class to register on LinkedIn and develop connections with business people in the community. While that may seem early to introduce students to a professional network, we believe this should be a natural part of their learning experience.

The job market has revealed that soft skills are in high demand—it's not just degrees and technical expertise that help you succeed after graduation. It's about knowing how to present yourself confidently, productively working well with others, and being able to adapt quickly to a fast-changing economy. Every student should be equipped with these skills well before they venture out into a world filled with jobs that didn't even exist when these students walked into their first classrooms.

We hope this book will help educators and faculty find new ways to inspire and empower their students to embrace the reality of the world today and change it for the better tomorrow.

PART I:
LAYING YOUR CAREER FOUNDATION

CHAPTER 1

WHAT IS LINKEDIN AND WHY USE IT?

Starting Your Journey

If you've ever been on LinkedIn, you've probably already realized what we're about to say. However, it's important to mention it anyway, so we can accept the truth and get past it quickly. LinkedIn was not made for students. The LinkedIn founders didn't create a tool or build a company to help students and schools. The primary source of membership and customers for LinkedIn is today's jobs, companies, and professionals, which is unlikely to change any time soon. This is why LinkedIn's mission has always been to make the world's professionals more productive and successful. Unfortunately, this strategy hasn't attracted many students, making them feel they don't belong on LinkedIn.

Fortunately, this doesn't matter, because this book is about making LinkedIn work for you regardless of where you are in your journey as a student or graduate.

Many students, universities, and even graduates view LinkedIn as a place to simply:

- copy and paste their online resumes/CVs
- search and apply for jobs

- connect with people they already know
- accept connection requests from people similar to them
- find basic company information

What most students don't realize is LinkedIn has the potential to help them connect and build relationships with their ideal future employers and to identify career opportunities while they're still in school. One doesn't need to have specific skills and experience to get started on LinkedIn, and the legal age to register on the platform is only 13. In other words, for you, the right time is *now*. By joining LinkedIn early, you will have access to trends in the job market and will be much better prepared to make the right choices once you graduate.

Why is this important?

This is important because as a student and graduate, you should know where you need to focus most of your time and effort to get the best career results. Not knowing this information is like throwing darts in the dark. You know there's a target in front of you, but you can't see it. You throw aimlessly, hoping all your darts land somewhere on the target and produce a good result.

LinkedIn's 2018 U.S. Emerging Jobs Report[1] lists the jobs and skills growing rapidly across America. LinkedIn amassed enough historical data and membership numbers to understand where people go when they move jobs, what they do when they get there, and how long they last in those jobs. In many ways, it's good to see where jobs are going and what skills you need to succeed in those jobs.

Never before have you had access to data and statistics that shine a light on exactly what skills are in highest demand and where you need to aim to increase your chances of success. No matter what you think of your chances to land your dream job, you can start making better and smarter decisions today.

---

1 LinkedIn, "LinkedIn 2018 Emerging Jobs Report," December 13, 2018, https://economicgraph.linkedin.com/research/linkedin-2018-emerging-jobs-report

What Is LinkedIn and Why Use It?

The Emerging Jobs Report reveals that the use of artificial intelligence (AI) continues to increase across many different sectors of the economy beyond just technology. Even if you're not looking to gain advanced AI skills, you should know enough about it to understand how it's changing your industry. Learn about how it might disrupt current jobs or create new opportunities you haven't even considered.

Another trend in the report reflects the growth of administrative, software engineer, account executive, and recruiter positions. Thus, underlying business and operational skills and experience will continue to be in demand for the foreseeable future.

LinkedIn has also published a list of the top companies people in the UK[2] and the US[3] want to work for in 2019. You'll see each company's fastest growing skills and job functions with the most new hires.

Don't worry if you're not interested in these technical and scientific roles. It doesn't mean you can't succeed in the future. If you look closely at these companies, you'll find many have departments of hundreds or thousands of employees with HR, sales, design, administrative, and project management responsibilities.

These LinkedIn articles also have links to the lists of top companies in Australia, United States, Canada, Japan, China, France, Germany, India, Mexico, and Brazil. You may find you don't care about any of these companies or jobs. But don't underestimate the value of understanding these trends to make wise decisions about the types of skills you need to develop that will lead to the most opportunities.

Perhaps unsurprisingly, one of the most significant skill gaps is soft skills. Everyone needs to have these skills to get a decent job in today's economy. Submitting a job application, having a call with a recruiter or

---

2 Katie Carroll, "Top Companies 2019: Where the UK Wants to Work Now," *LinkedIn,* April 2, 2019, https://www.linkedin.com/pulse/top-companies-2019-where-uk-wants-work-now-katie-carroll

3 Daniel Roth, "Top Companies 2019: Where the U.S. Wants to Work Now," *LinkedIn,* https://www.linkedin.com/pulse/top-companies-2019-where-us-wants-work-now-daniel-roth

hiring manager, and attending an onsite interview are all standard means employers use to detect whether candidates have excellent soft skills.

Yet, going through these essential job search steps, many recent graduates struggle to demonstrate what matters most. If you ask employers what they look for, they'll often say they want students to clearly demonstrate the relevance of the skills they've gained through their studies and especially through extra-curricular work. Problem-solving, self-management, and team work are prominent among the skills many employers believe students and graduates lack to succeed in today's workplace.

You can find many ways to stand out in the crowded job market without having any paid work experience. Join your student union, student government, or any other clubs, societies, and groups. These activities can help you develop valuable leadership, project management, event management, budgeting, communication, and networking skills.[4] Treat these experiences as any other work experience even if you acquired them during your university years.

When looking at the importance of hard skills vs. soft skills, 57% of business leaders say soft skills are more important than hard skills.[5] This is good news for students and graduates who sometimes feel they can't get the jobs they want due to a lack of work experience. Your future boss may be more interested in seeing your soft skills than your wizardry with apps, software, and online tools, which they expect you to possess anyway.

---

4 Frances Trought, *Brilliant Employability Skills: How to Stand Out from the Crowd in the Graduate Job Market,* (Harlow: Pearson Education Limited, 2012), 3-13

5 Gregory Lewis, "The Most In-Demand Hard Skills and Soft Skills of 2019," *LinkedIn,* January 3, 2019, https://business.linkedin.com/talent-solutions/blog/trends-and-research/2018/the-most-in-demand-hard-and-soft-skills-of-2018

ESSENTIAL SOFT SKILLS FOR CAREER BUILDING

Soft skills are about your behavior or thinking – your personal characteristics and cognitive skills. Note that soft skills make up about 25% of the skills required to do most jobs.

Creativity
Using your imagination to come up with original ideas and unconventional ways of doing things, it can be honed – if you work at it.

Persuasion
understanding your audience's perspective on a situation, empathizing with their pain points and communicating the value of your solution.

Time management
working efficiently and effectively to meet deadlines consistently.

Problem-solving
being able to recognize challenges, identify potential solutions and implement the most fitting solution.

Communication
actively listening and being aware of non-verbal communication, such as eye contact, body language and facial expressions.

Self-management
taking responsibility for your own actions, showing initiative and being organized and accountable.

Collaboration
working with others to achieve a goal in an environment of cooperation and mutual respect.

Adaptability
being able to grow, evolve and move into different roles as the situation or company changes.

Even if you feel you've got valuable work experience as a student or graduate, please don't disregard even the smallest and simplest steps—they matter more than you think! Can you follow directions and make sure you attach a PDF copy of your cover letter and resume and send it to the right person? Can you present yourself professionally on the phone and make sure you've researched the position you are interviewing for and organization well before the call? Are you ready to walk into the office of your dream job and convince the interviewing committee you have what it takes to be a successful employee?

These pieces of advice may all seem basic, but unfortunately, we've seen students and graduates miss out on opportunities because they didn't consider the importance of getting the basics right and making a great impression before they ever walk through the door. You have to demonstrate you're the right person for the job in every step of the hiring process.

If you have strong organizational, time management, and oral communication skills, you already have some of the essentials needed for this journey. But don't forget: a negative attitude or inauthentic vibe will neutralize any positive qualities you may have.

We hope this helps you understand why it's becoming increasingly important to start thinking like a professional early in your student journey. The good news is it's never been easier to access tools, information, and ways of learning you can adapt to your needs and your future career. You no longer have to depend only on your academic performance or the recommendations of your parents and teachers. You have access to people, tools and information on the web (and on your phone!) beyond what your parents or teachers could even imagine when they were in school. Don't hold it against them if they don't get it. And maybe this book will help both you and them see this new world of possibilities in a new light.

TOP 11 JOB INTERVIEW MISTAKES

You need to start seeing LinkedIn as an opportunity to:

- showcase your personal and professional brand so you can stand out from the crowd
- find influencers and decision-makers doing the work you love
- engage your network by sharing valuable professional content

- build strong relationships that will open doors you didn't know existed

If you're using Facebook, Instagram, Twitter, YouTube, or any other social site, you're already showcasing your personal brand. Your brand is essentially your reputation—what people say about you when you're not in the room and what you're known for based on the things you share and the way you act.

On LinkedIn, this is called your professional brand. The clear distinction is that not everything that is part of your personal brand is useful or appropriate for a professional network, such as LinkedIn. Some people will think of this differently, but as a student or graduate, you need to keep these distinctions clear.

Here's an easy rule to follow when considering sharing something on LinkedIn: would you share it during a professional meeting or job interview? If not, it's probably best to keep it off LinkedIn.

The word *professional* might put you off because it signifies being part of a profession or doing paid work, but we believe any student can have a professional brand. The work, activities, and projects you do in school can contribute to it. It can also include your job interests and any volunteer experience you may have.

Your LinkedIn profile can be made up of all of these, and just like employees celebrate achievements on LinkedIn, such as promotions and new jobs, you can also highlight your own academic achievements that align with your professional interests. The rule here is that if you're proud to share your school achievements with friends and family, they probably belong on your LinkedIn profile. We'll discuss where and how to share your academic accomplishments in later chapters.

Since opportunities are tied to people, you'll want to identify the influencers and decision-makers on LinkedIn so you can connect with them. The influencers are usually people who are highly visible and recognized as leaders and experts in their respective fields. Those influencers aren't limited to names such as Jeff Bezos or Bill Gates. Fame doesn't necessarily equal influence—at least not the kind you need.

These people can also be local leaders well known in your community, experts you admire, or authors you enjoy reading. Ask yourself: who are the people doing the work you love?

When it comes to decision-makers, we mean people such as recruiters and hiring managers. You can almost guarantee they will be on LinkedIn, looking for the right candidates. In later chapters, you'll learn how they think, what tactics they use, and how to approach or attract them—even when you don't think you're qualified enough.

LinkedIn isn't just the place to showcase yourself or find influential people. It's also the perfect place to engage with your network. This means staying in touch with your connections by liking, sharing, and commenting on their updates. Sounds like something you've probably been doing for a long time, right? But now, you have to think in the context of a professional network: the people and companies who will hire you in the future. LinkedIn is the perfect place to explore their profiles and see what they like and what they care about. You might just end up starting a conversation with your future boss! How exciting is that?

From now on, see LinkedIn as the best place to build strong relationships with the types of people you want to work with and the companies you want to work for. It's no longer enough just to go through companies' websites and online applications to understand what your future employers care about. LinkedIn can be the best chance you have to get to know your potential employers before you ever meet them in person. And that means you'll be better prepared to get a job you desire than the vast majority of students and graduates out there.

These relationships will help you uncover information and opportunities you can't get any other way. Imagine building a relationship with a respected engineer who ends up referring you to your dream job, all because you sent a connection request and respectfully asked for 15 minutes of their time to discuss something you're both passionate about. It happens all the time, but it only happens to people who understand and take advantage of the real potential of LinkedIn.

University Pages and Alumni Tool

On LinkedIn, universities have their own pages with an overview of who they are and what they offer. Go ahead and search for yours on LinkedIn. You can find alumni and employee networks with career insights, providing you with valuable information about professionals who have attended your university or currently work there.

You'll be able to see where alumni live, where they work, what they studied, what skills they have, and what they do for their organizations. Imagine what you could do with this information! With LinkedIn, you can search by dates they attended the school or the year they graduated from it, their titles, keywords from their profiles, or the companies they work for. This will make it even easier to focus on what you care about.

Let's say you're interested in working in media and communications in New York City, but you're not sure about the best approach to finding a great career there. Thankfully, the alumni tool can offer you just what you need to get started. It will show you the exact number of alumni who live in New York City and work in that industry as well as their professional backgrounds. Now, you have a list of great people and companies you can research and learn from so that you can make smart career decisions. Most alumni love helping students from their universities, so why wouldn't you reach out to them?

We'll talk later about the best ways to connect and message alumni. For now, make sure you take some time to explore your university page and get comfortable using the alumni tool. It's the beginning of your journey through LinkedIn.

What Is LinkedIn and Why Use It

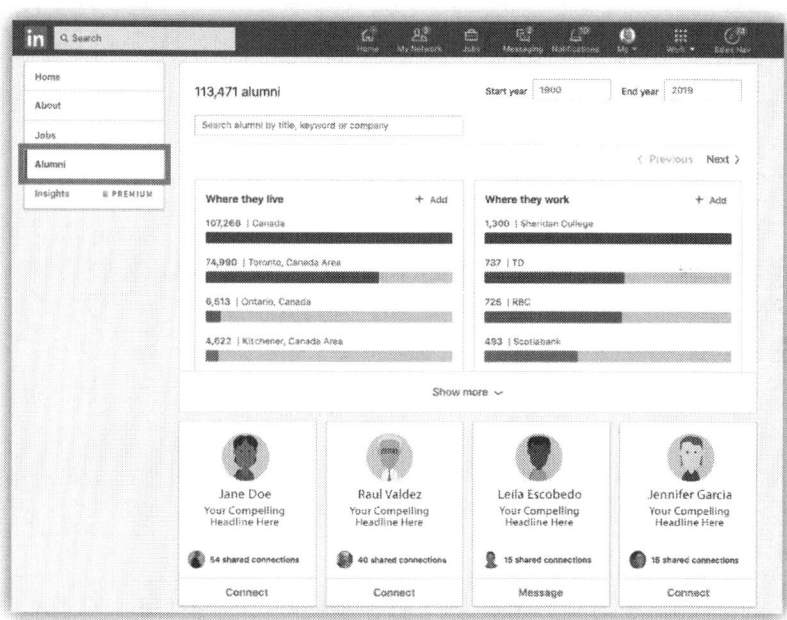

ation for Students to Get Started

The following stories are shared by Miguel to inspire you to pursue your dream career with confidence with the help of LinkedIn.

"Over the past ten years, I've had the pleasure of working with thousands of students, ranging from high school to MBA and Ph.D. programs. In that time, I've been fortunate to see young individuals go through truly transformative experiences that have changed the way they see themselves and whom they ultimately wish to become. While I can't say all of them used LinkedIn to succeed, I *can* tell you that all of them went above and beyond their academic experience and left their comfort zones to achieve more than they thought possible.

One of those students was a young lady named Kristen. At the age of 22, Kristen moved from New York to Bangkok with just two suitcases and a degree in theatre. She quickly created a niche for herself in the performing arts industry, where she was contracted to sing jazz for luxury hotels around Southeast Asia. Kristen believes much of her success in winning contracts was due to the conversations she started with hotel managers on LinkedIn.

She began by looking up luxury hotels in major cities, such as Hong Kong and Singapore. After looking at the hotel's website to make sure it offered live music to their guests, she turned to LinkedIn to search for the relevant members of staff with whom she could get in touch. Kristen searched for employees with the titles General Manager or Food and Beverage Manager. Once she found them, she asked to connect with the aim of starting a conversation. Although Kristen didn't always end up with a contract, she usually created opportunities to network, make connections, and learn more about the local culture and industry.

After her travels in Asia, Kristen decided to pursue an MBA at the University of Warwick (WBS) in the United Kingdom. Despite pursuing a different career, Kristen continues to apply a similar approach in her current job search. Whenever she thinks of a company and role she's interested in, she searches for people on LinkedIn that fit that profile. Kristen is savvy enough to know that the best way to understand potential career paths is to understand people who are already on those paths and who have a mix of experiences working in different roles and companies. She continues to send connection requests to professionals with whom she would like to speak in hopes they can give her a better understanding of what the next steps could be in pursuing a specific role.

Kristen also turns to LinkedIn before professional events and lectures by visiting speakers. She researches the speakers and usually contacts one or two whose career paths match her interests. This approach allows her to not only follow up with key influencers and industry leaders after the event but also remain in touch with them for months and years to come. She knows every connection she makes has the potential to make her career dream a reality.

Back when I started running my workshops for universities, I came across many students who either didn't have LinkedIn profiles or had barely filled out their profiles. Lori was one of them. She was studying translation but didn't know what her career path would look like. From the beginning, I could tell Lori was a creative, passionate person. Once I helped her set up the basics of her profile, Lori began to spread her wings and fly to new heights.

In the About section of her LinkedIn profile, Lori beautifully described the intersection of her love for languages, technology, and media. She knew that to be unique and to prepare for the future, she needed to demonstrate she had a deep interest and broad experience, combining different disciplines and bringing together seemingly unrelated concepts in ways that were changing the translation industry.

Lori brought her work to life by publishing an article on LinkedIn, where she argued why human translators wouldn't be replaced by machines because of cultural differences and words and concepts that don't exist in another language. Although technology could help, Lori was aware of its limits. In a few weeks, Lori had gone from barely having a LinkedIn profile to someone who was telling stories that shined a light on her skills, personality, knowledge, and experience. While she didn't get thousands of likes on her article, she *did* attract the attention of leaders working in translation and artificial intelligence, who added their own thoughts in the comments section of her article. It was a fantastic thing to see.

After graduating, Lori was able to secure numerous opportunities as a freelancer, working on films, shows, and documentaries, creating and proofreading subtitles. I remember the day she published her first article on LinkedIn and how proud I was that she put herself out there when so many other students were afraid or unwilling to do the same. Lori didn't let her inexperience get in the way of sharing her voice on LinkedIn. Now, any time a future employer looks at her profile, they'll be able to see Lori means business.

Finally, I want to tell you about Filip, who was one of the most amazing students I've ever worked with. I say that because he applied everything he learned in ways that produced significant results even though he had zero work experience in his desired field. During Filip's final year at university, he decided not to pursue a career in academia—a departure from his original intention.

Most of Filip's experience consisted of lab research. He realized it wasn't what most employers were looking for. This made him feel very anxious as he approached graduation with few (if any) job prospects. During this time, I met Filip while he was attending the LinkedIn program I ran at his university. Almost immediately, he felt inspired by the videos and stories I shared during that first workshop. He realized there was a light at the end of the tunnel for people in his situation.

Several workshops later, Filip was using LinkedIn to research the careers of people whose interests were similar to his. He wanted to connect with them to leverage their personal wisdom that wouldn't be available anywhere else. He made a list of all their companies and visited many relevant sites, gathering even more information. Next, he narrowed down the list and decided to reach out to a few people from each company with a personalized message. He told them about his desire to seek out wisdom, asking them if they would be willing to have a chat over coffee.

To Filip's surprise and delight, most people were happy to help. He ended up meeting people from multiple companies, getting valuable advice about the industry. He also learned about additional job openings he hadn't considered before. Eventually, Filip gained the courage to reach out to the CEO of a small company he knew was looking for help on a short part-time project. One Skype interview later, Filip was offered the position. The experience served to further boost his confidence.

In just over six months, with the help of LinkedIn, Filip overcame his anxiety about his lack of experience. He went from not knowing the job

What Is LinkedIn and Why Use It?

market to building multiple senior-level relationships in his field, accepting two paid job positions and a potential third job offer that promises to be even more exciting."

Kristen

> Searched for relevant companies, decision makers, mentors and industry influencers.

> Built relationships with those decision makers, mentors and industry influencers, which led to opportunities.

Lori

> Wrote and posted LinkedIn Publisher articles, shining a light on her skills, personality, knowledge and experience.

> Had conversations with industry leaders who engaged with her articles.

Filip

> Researched, connected and started relationships with peers and mentors doing jobs that interested him.

> Researched companies of interest and then connected with decision makers about potential positions.

The same, if not better, is possible for you!

Don't underestimate the power of LinkedIn at any point in your student and graduate journey. Whether you start early as a student or have already graduated, this is the time to discover what you really love doing. This is the time to put yourself out there. You don't have to merely rely on books or assumptions you've made about what your career should look like. With

LinkedIn, you can go directly to the sources of knowledge—the professionals—to find out what it's really like to work in your chosen field and profession. Just remember that each and every professional you meet on LinkedIn is a step toward building a network that will be there to support you during the inevitable highs and lows of your career.

We're not here to tell you that LinkedIn will have all the answers for you, but we *can* guarantee it will have enough of them to get you moving in the right direction. We're writing this because we've seen how students even with extremely low confidence, mental health issues, and chronic financial difficulties have been able to overcome these challenges by finding opportunities through their professional networks. Many older adults have been doing this for a very long time before LinkedIn—or the Internet, for that matter—ever existed. You're lucky enough to have the best tool available to do it smarter and faster.

What are you waiting for?

Things to focus on in the next seven days:

1. Write specific goals for using LinkedIn during the next 3-12 months.
2. Search for the type of jobs available in your job market.
3. Understand what skills are in demand in your job market.

Things to start doing in the next seven days:

1. Search for three jobs related to your interests on LinkedIn.
2. Make a list of the top 10 skills listed in the job descriptions.
3. Find alumni on LinkedIn with the jobs and skills you've discovered.

CHAPTER 2

DEFINING WHO YOU ARE AND WHOM YOU WANT TO BECOME

Now that you have a good understanding of the enormous potential LinkedIn can offer you as a student or graduate, we want to spend some time helping you understand yourself and what you'd like to achieve in the next few years. The topics in this chapter are essential because they will form the guidelines for your use of LinkedIn.

We don't believe in the one-size-fits-all approach, so we want to make sure you know what'll work best for you and where you'll need the most help. That's why we'll ask you questions making you think rather than handing you a map with all the landmarks and routes laid out. This is the time to gain a deeper understanding of yourself above all else.

Follow Your Passion

Defining who you are is the first step we'd like you to think about—meaning the way you would describe yourself to others.

Let's start with the following question: what are you passionate about?

Is that a hard question for you to answer in 30 seconds or less? If you struggle to provide an answer, don't feel bad. Most students (and even professionals) we've worked with can't clearly define their passions either. While this may not seem as a big problem now, it can become a barrier once you leave university. You might end up with people influencing your decisions in ways that are not in your best interests.

> *"Passion exists at the intersection of three or more things you're really curious about."*
>
> – Steven Kotler[6]

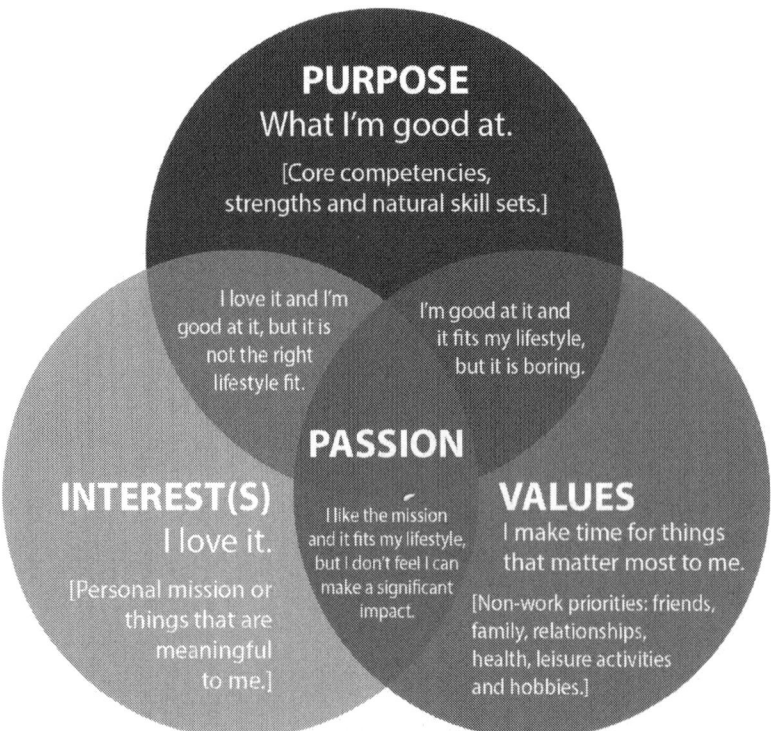

We want to encourage you to simplify the process of figuring out your passion. What are the topics you're most curious about?

Make a list of the top ten, and write a short description for each.

---

6 Steven Kotler, "The Passion Recipe: Four Steps to Total Fulfilment," *Forbes*, March 27, 2015, https://www.forbes.com/sites/stevenkotler/2015/03/27/the-passion-recipe-four-steps-to-total-fulfillment

For example, what kind of issue would have you glued to the TV even if it was a three-hour documentary? What could you work on for a whole year, or even a few years, without getting bored and without getting much recognition? If you could spend your life solving some of the world's most significant problems without having to worry about money, what would they be?

Once you have your list of ten topics, it's time to start prioritizing. You want to end up with topics most important to you, where you have the most relevant skills and/or experience, and the most pertinent to specific needs in the job market.

Here's an example of some of ours, in no particular order:

1. Youth unemployment and underemployment
2. The loss of jobs to automation and technology
3. The global economy and international relations
4. Applying entrepreneurship to one's career
5. Technology and social media in education
6. Learning and development
7. Effective storytelling in business
8. Wellness and wellbeing at work
9. Balancing being a parent and an earner
10. Coaching and leadership best practices

All these topics are important to us at a professional and personal level. Our deep curiosity in these topics have led us both to live a life of meaning, and they have helped align our career choices with our values.

Now, here's a condensed version of themes from the list above:

1. Education
2. Entrepreneurship
3. Technology

Our most meaningful, energetic, and productive work will happen at the intersection of these themes. It's no accident that what we both do for a living today involves all three of these areas.

We hope this short exercise has helped you see that you can be curious and passionate about many different topics and still be able to find a career at the intersection of the ones you prioritize. Actually, some of the most critical jobs in the world require a multidisciplinary approach, and the more technology changes the way we work, the more important this will become.

In his book *The Start-Up of You,* Reid Hoffmann, a co-founder of LinkedIn, compares the entrepreneurial mindset and ways of working in the tech/start-up industry to the way he thinks everyone should operate in their careers.[7] He suggests we should all be in a permanent beta testing mode, considering ourselves never-ending works in progress. Each day is an opportunity to do more, learn more, and grow more. Once you adopt this mindset, you force yourself to acknowledge your "bugs" and discover what you need to improve so you can adapt and evolve. Hoffmann tells us that developing our competitive advantage means combining our assets, aspirations, and the market realities.

In the same way, developing our passion is a never-ending process. You don't need to wait for it to be clear and refined. Quite the opposite, you need to start and keep moving forward even if it takes you several jobs to find the best fit.

Along your journey, you'll find plenty of people who don't believe in this whole passion stuff. They'll want you to be practical and stick to the tried and tested paths.

In his book *Do What You Want,* author Nicholas Bate has the following words of advice to help you deal with these negative attitudes: stop worrying about what other people think, live in the present, don't plan just for the future, look for the intrinsic worth of any job, and understand your value. Bate provides a personal compass as a guide to everything that matters in your life's journey: career, wellness, personal finance, relationships, social contribution, and fun.

---

7 Reid Hoffman, *The Start-Up of You: Adapt to the Future, Invest in Yourself and Transform Your Career,* (New York: Currency, 2012), 21-23

What struck us the most in Bate's book is the fact that he reminds us we can no longer consider our careers without the full contexts of our lives.[8] No matter what you decide, remember: the career you choose will make or break all other important areas of your life. This is exactly why you can't solely rely on your parents, teachers, and best friends to show you the way—no one knows you as well as you do.

Passion Turned into Purpose

To illustrate our next topic, Miguel would like to share part of his journey to finding his ideal career:

"During my high school years in McAllen, Texas, I spent a few days a week after school helping students apply for college as part of a program for disadvantaged youth in our community.

While I was at university, I lobbied my state government in Austin, Texas, to maintain grant funding levels for first-generation students—those who were the first from their families to attend a college or university. This was all before I turned 20.

In my 20s, as part of my career, using technology and social media, I helped thousands of students, graduates, and school staff.

As I am co-authoring this book, I hope I can help millions. Simply put, I turned my passion into purpose each step of the way by finding people I could help and problems I could solve. My journey has led me to make enough money to raise a family abroad, travel the world, and live a comfortable life in London while my co-author has relocated from Canada to Amsterdam. This is our version of success up to this point.

I share this with you because I want you to look back at your own life and find experiences that can translate to career success. Think about any volunteering programs, activities, events, campaigns, and projects you've been involved in that highlight how you turned your passion into purpose.

---

8 Nicholas Bate, *Do What You Want: The Book that Shows You How to Create a Career You'll Love*, (Toronto: Pearson Education Canada, 2012), 117-130

It doesn't need to be big and flashy stuff—just moments where you made a difference, shaping you into the kind of person you are now and the professional you will become. It might just be enough to convince recruiters and hiring managers that you have the right attitude and learning capacity to do the job. Who said you didn't have enough skills and experience? Your story of how you've turned your passion into purpose can be enough to get your foot in the door."

We recommend you watch "How to Find Your Passion" by Jason Silva from the YouTube channel Shots of Awe.[9] In the video, Jason does a great job of simplifying and electrifying this topic. If you enjoy it, we recommend you look at some of his other videos, dealing with meaningful issues and questions we all face in life.

Find a Career Aligned with Your Values

Another factor that's shaped you is your values. These are the principles and standards that drive your behavior and judgment of what's important in life. We can refer to them as moral principles and ethics ingrained in us from an early age by parents, teachers, authority figures, and other people we admire.

Often, the reason why many employees feel disengaged from their work is because their work doesn't align with their passion and values. Of course, many will argue that it's not always possible to find the kind of work they want, and we truly sympathize with them if they've struggled for many years to find a great job regardless of their best intentions and efforts. But we encourage you not to think this way, especially if you haven't spent any time in the job market.

As a student or graduate, you need to consider your values when thinking seriously about your ideal career. Before you think about prestige, benefits, and salary, you need to consider your personality, values, and cultural fit to decide whether you'd be happy and prosperous in a particular career. Later in this book, we'll explore how you can use LinkedIn to help you find some

---

9 Jason Silva: Shots of Awe, "How to Find Your Passion," *YouTube* video, 2:11, June 7, 2016, https://www.youtube.com/watch?v=HScOL_aOMrw

of the answers to these questions. For now, read what Miguel did to figure out where he fit:

"I studied political science and international relations, but halfway through graduate school, I started realizing there weren't many jobs and organizations related to my studies that I could see myself working in. What did I do? I started looking for jobs in the tech industry, where who I was (passion and values) aligned with whom I wanted to become (skills and ambition).

With the help of just a single event at a small startup, I found the way into my first job in tech as an unpaid intern and social media manager. Here, I ended up meeting and working with hundreds of entrepreneurs, which eventually led me to my next job. Yes, I started at the bottom, but it was the bottom of something I loved doing. Thanks to having the foresight to see the summit of my ideal career, the climb has been fantastic ever since."

What Does It Mean to Have a Fulfilling Career?

A great blog worth following—www.lifehack.org—is dedicated to a range of different topics on solving life's challenges, big or small, with both smart and simple approaches. One of its articles, titled "How to Find Your Ideal Career Path Without Wasting Time on Jobs Not Suitable for You" by Jenny Marchal, focuses on the number one killer of happiness, productivity, and sanity: choosing a job that's not meant for you and making a long, miserable career out of it.

Marchal talks about the main things you should consider when choosing the right career, for example: do what excites and energizes you, think about what you're already good at, don't limit yourself to thinking about a specific job, research qualifications required, and get to know the people in that field. The best message of all is never let anyone deter you from believing you can find a fulfilling career for there is something out there for everyone.[10]

---

10 Jenny Marchal, "How to Find Your Ideal Career Path Without Wasting Time on Jobs Not Suitable for You," *Lifehack*, https://www.lifehack.org/585462/how-decide-career

Six values that resonate with most people help nurture a joyful work environment: learning, openness, love, meaning, participation, and positivity.[11]

When considering a new workplace, attempt to answer the following questions:

- What does onboarding look like at this company, and what training is offered to new employees?
- How diverse is the company when it comes to age, race, and gender?
- Does it seem people love what they do at this company?
- How will you in your new role contribute to the organization's overall vision and mission?
- Is collaboration encouraged in the workplace?
- Is there an optimistic mood around the company?

You may be wondering how you would ever be able to answer these questions as a job candidate—it's rarely easy. That's why LinkedIn will be your best friend when it comes to knowing your future employer.

Things to focus on in the next seven days:

1. What would get you excited about going to work, and how would you know you're successful?
2. What are some things you would never be able to compromise on when deciding what jobs fit you best?
3. What areas of your life matter to you as much, or more, as your career?

---

11 Sophie Rowan, *Brilliant Career Coach: How to Find and Follow Your Dream Career*, (Harlow: Pearson Education Limited, 2011), 56-58

Things to start doing in the next seven days:

1. Research the best companies to work for across the web, and start following them on LinkedIn.

2. See what language those companies use to describe their cultures and values, and make a list of those that matter to you the most.

3. Check what other perks and benefits these companies offer, and make a list of those that matter to you the most.

CHAPTER 3

TURNING STUDENTS INTO SOUGHT-AFTER PROFESSIONALS

The world of work changes at such a high speed that even experienced professionals have to continually learn and adapt to remain competitive in their careers. You need to pay close attention to this trend, taking place across most of the job markets. In a way, we all need to remain students throughout our lives, and while that may seem to clash with the core message of this chapter, it actually represents the beauty of the concepts we cover here.

We want you to feel confident in yourself as a student or recent graduate. To accomplish that, you need to start thinking, looking, and acting as a professional, regardless of how you currently feel. It's perfectly okay to have doubts and feel anxious about your career prospects, but you'll need to put those thoughts aside so you can focus on what it takes to become the kind of professional you want (and need) to be. A good first step is to take some time to survey the people from the professions you're interested in.

For example, many professionals in our chosen industry, companies, and functions have:

- graduate and post-graduate degrees
- background in financial services
- analytical skills and project management certifications
- high-paying jobs in New York City, Los Angeles, and San Francisco

- 5-10+ years' experience working for one company
- salaries averaging $120,000
- first jobs as analysts or associate researchers.

This is by no means an exhaustive list of what to look for, but it also does not mean you need to copy other professionals to be successful. The list above is an example, meant to help you identify the professionals in the job market whose jobs most closely match the work you want to do. Once you research these professionals, you'll start getting a better sense of what you'll need for your own professional journey on LinkedIn. In later chapters, we'll cover what to look for in these professionals' LinkedIn profiles to understand how to advance in your chosen career.

Indispensable Skills for Any Career

The good news about being a professional is that many of the skills and habits involved require zero special talents. Seriously! You don't need a degree or specialized certification to get these things right. You merely need to recognize them and practice them as much as possible so they become second nature. It also helps to spend time with like-minded people to spur you on.

Here are 15 easy things you can do to start thinking, looking, and acting like a professional:

1. be prepared
2. have a strong work ethic
3. be willing to learn
4. demonstrate high energy
5. have a good attitude
6. go above and beyond the call of duty
7. show your passion
8. be flexible
9. use positive body language
10. be punctual

11. ask for advice
12. focus on finishing tasks
13. seek to collaborate with others
14. accept mistakes and learn from them
15. ask questions.

We can't stress enough how simple but important these actions and attitudes are in any professional situation. Although following this advice won't necessarily set you apart from other job candidates or help you get to the top of the list, not following it can jeopardize your opportunity to get a job or advance your career.

You also need to consider soft skills. Every professional needs to have them in their toolbox. Soft skills are the essential abilities every hiring manager looks for, and they will help you stand out as a recent graduate if you can demonstrate how you've used them in the past.

Soft skills include:
- setting and achieving goals
- time management
- staying organized in difficult situations
- self-awareness
- being a self-starter
- managing feedback constructively
- public speaking
- effective listening
- communicating effectively
- influencing others
- thinking critically and problem solving
- collaborating on projects
- resilience
- adaptability.

Now, think of other soft skills you might have, and write a few examples of how you can demonstrate each or how you plan to develop them.

Having a busy student life shouldn't get in the way of learning the basics you'll need as a professional in the world of work. In a perfect world, many of your courses and assignments would already be helping you develop these skills. However, in our experience, this type of training doesn't always happen in universities, and many students graduate without a firm grasp of basic professional skills. It's disheartening to see students and graduates struggling to get the internships and jobs they want because they fail to communicate with confidence or lack clarity when discussing examples of their professional experience.

Here's a story Miguel often shares in his workshops to highlight this point.

Making a Bad Impression

About ten minutes into one of my university workshops, a young lady strolled into the room, looking very anxious. Having seen many late walk-ins throughout my career, I kept presenting to the audience, assuming she would find an empty seat. I was wrong. Instead of sitting down, this young lady hovered around the back of the room, looking down at the floor with her arms crossed and her bag held tightly to her side. I could tell she was uncomfortable because she arrived late, but it also appeared that she was inexplicably nervous as though she was in some sort of trouble.

I paused, welcomed her, and pointed out a few seats available in the front of the room. I thought this would be enough to help her find a chair, so I returned to my lecture. Turns out I was wrong… again! Instead of sitting in one of the empty seats, the young lady slowly made her way to the front and stood awkwardly to the side of the podium where I was presenting. Now I had no choice but to stop my presentation as the audience was distracted, likely wondering what she was doing. Although I'm usually known for my calm and collected demeanor, I'm sure my face betrayed my confusion when I stopped presenting again.

I turned to her and attempted a smile, asking if she needed something else. She came closer to me and whispered that she didn't know where to sit because she didn't know anyone in the room. *What?* My jaw dropped—at least figuratively—as I could not believe what I heard. In my best effort to make light of the situation while remaining encouraging, I smiled and whispered back, pointing out the fact that almost no one in the room knew anybody else before coming to this first workshop. After all, this was a university of over 30,000 students in the heart of London! Finally, another student pulled out a chair, offering her a seat at their table. That was all that was needed for her to sit down. She did not say a word for the rest of the workshop and didn't participate in any activities. I never saw her again.

This memory always makes me sad because I wasn't able to help a student who was probably struggling with something I could not fully understand. Most likely, it was her introversion and intense social anxiety that made it difficult for her to walk into a room full of strangers. At least I hope so!

The reason I share this story is that over the years, I've met many other students who struggled with the same things to varying degrees. Most were students who weren't able to introduce themselves appropriately, listen and communicate effectively, present with confidence, or collaborate productively in groups. These were not just high school or undergraduate students—they were graduate and Ph.D. and MBA students, who seemed to lack basic interpersonal skills. I was taking them out of their comfort zones, away from lectures and screens, and it became clear to me there was a vast disconnect between the academic and professional worlds. While I strive to be very accepting and understanding of every student in my workshops, I knew from experience that employers would have much less patience.

Managing Your Blind Spots

Throughout my workshops, I kept noticing these gaps in professional knowledge and behavior of my students. What makes it even more difficult is students often don't realize they're holding themselves back although they're doing what's required of them: finishing their assignments, studying for their exams, and passing on to the next year until they graduate. Sadly, this hasn't been enough for a long time, but we still keep falling into the same traps.

The blame doesn't lie with one person or department; it's the way most schools prioritize their curricula and standardized testing above ensuring students have relevant professional skills. But we're not interested in assigning blame in this book. Instead, I want to help you gain a level of professional self-awareness that will help you avoid your student blind spots.

Wait... before we move on: were you aware you had blind spots?

Many students I work with have no idea they lack the basic but essential skills expected of them. Instead, they worry mostly about having little or no work experience to put on their resumes. The extent of career-related help they receive from their universities is typically limited to choosing resume templates, support with writing and editing, filling out applications, and attending generic mock interviews and overwhelming job fairs. However, this is only 1% of what you need to master—the other 99% usually isn't provided by any one person, event, or academic department. To become a professional, you'll need to take things into your own hands and not become overly dependent on others for guidance, just like you'll have to do for much of your professional life.

How exactly do you discover the things you don't know you don't know? How do you identify the inevitable blind spots accompanying you in your student life?

Simply put, you'll need to start working instead of just studying. It's time to create your own professional plan and calendar. It might feel like a lot of extra work, but stick with it because the transformation of your student life will be amazing!

Here's how to start:

1. Set up a new email address for professional purposes with your first and last name, and keep it separate from your student email. For example, firstname.lastname@gmail.com.

2. Try to buy a domain name with your own name, e.g., EmilyAngelaJones.com, for a low yearly fee, and renew each year. You can buy a domain from a few dollars up to $12-15 a year. (Some of the best website creation sites we've tried are Wix.com, Squarespace.com, Wordpress.com, and GoDaddy.com.)

3. Use a simple website creator to create your landing page, and have fun with it! You'll be updating it on a regular basis, and no coding skills are required.

4. Set up your professional calendar with reminders to take courses, attend events, and meet other professionals in your chosen industry, outside your academic responsibilities. Consider color coding your calendar so you can quickly see what you're up to each week and month. You'll also use the calendar and associated information to send invites and set up calls and meetings.

5. Subscribe to free industry and company newsletters, download news apps, and set up alerts and notifications for specific topics. Follow the blogs and social media channels of your favorite industry influencers, and start sharing your favorite content with your LinkedIn network. You'll find the small LinkedIn "In" logo on most news sites and blogs these days to make social sharing easy.

The new email address will help you keep your personal and academic lives separate from your professional life. It's easy to switch from one email account to another using a single app on your phone. Plus, it might be less overwhelming than going through all the emails in your university inbox!

Purchasing a domain name will give you ownership of your identity and online brand. It's a unique way to showcase yourself in addition to the usual resume and cover letter combo, and employers will appreciate the effort when they review your portfolio.

Similarly, with your new email address, you'll want to have a new calendar category that aligns with your professional plan. This will keep you honest and organized. You can set up tasks and reminders outside of your school work, e.g., taking an online course to improve your public speaking, setting up a coffee meeting with a product designer you admire, or attending an artificial intelligence convention happening near you.

Finally, you'll want to use that new email address to sign up for activities relevant to your professional plan. You will want to be selective about with whom you share your email so that the information you receive in your inbox stays relevant to your mission and doesn't become a distraction.

As you take these steps, you should start coming across a multitude of new content, topics, groups, and people. It will begin to change the way you see your chosen profession and the world of work. You're opening yourself up to an external world that will reinforce, challenge, or contradict what you have learned at school. It might also present entirely new areas for you to explore that might change the course of your education. Taking the initiative to prepare for your professional journey earlier rather than later will help you navigate your career path with purpose as you make some of the most important decisions of your life.

Setting Yourself Up for Success

So far, we've explored what to look for when researching the professionals in your chosen career, developing the soft skills every professional requires, and avoiding your student blind spots by focusing on your approach to succeed outside of your academic requirements. The combination of these best practices will make you think, look, and act like a professional, making you stand out from the crowd. Even so, you should also be thinking of the power of the crowd to take your success even further.

Creating a quality network can mean many things, but here we're looking at building relationships with other professionals you admire. They don't need to be famous leaders or senior executives. They can be anyone in your chosen industry or organization as long as they can give you insights into what a career in that industry or company would look like.

No matter where you are in your student journey, you should get to a point where you are comfortable connecting and meeting with these professionals regularly. Sometimes, all it takes is connecting on LinkedIn and sending a short message to begin a conversation that could change your career unlike anything else you're doing in the lab or classroom.

Want a super easy way to start networking if you're a student? Focus on networking *inside* your university. Speak to other professors whom you've never met, spend time meeting administrative staff to learn about their work, and join student clubs and groups. You might be able to find them on LinkedIn!

Things to focus on in the next seven days:

1. What are the overarching patterns or similarities of professionals in your chosen field?
2. What three soft skills do you need to develop the most and how will you do it?
3. What do you struggle with that may prevent you from getting the job you want?

Things to start doing in the next seven days:

1. Manage your new email inbox and calendar separate from your university communications, and fill it with learning and networking opportunities not offered at your university.
2. Select projects, artwork, images, videos, and other interesting content you're proud of, and add it to your media section on your LinkedIn profile—make sure to add a description of each.
3. Seek out honest feedback on what you need to improve to help you find your dream career—ask people you trust and other professionals you meet. Listen carefully without judgement, ask for clarification if needed, and write down exactly what you hear.

CHAPTER 4

LINKEDIN ETIQUETTE AND BEST PRACTICES

So far, we've shared a few ideas and best practices to help you establish the foundations of your success on LinkedIn. The reason so many students give up on LinkedIn is they approach it without much purpose or motivation. We hope the last few chapters helped you define yours and develop an action plan you can now implement.

But before you spend time building your profile or engaging with your network, we want to make sure you know LinkedIn's etiquette and best practices as well as considerations for your LinkedIn strategy as a student or recent graduate.

Put Your Best Foot Forward Online

Do a simple Google search of your name. What comes up? Note the websites, links, and images attached to your name. Where do they lead? What do they represent? Are you happy with the results? If someone who's never met you came across this information, would they have a good understanding of who you are? Would they be impressed, or would they judge you negatively?

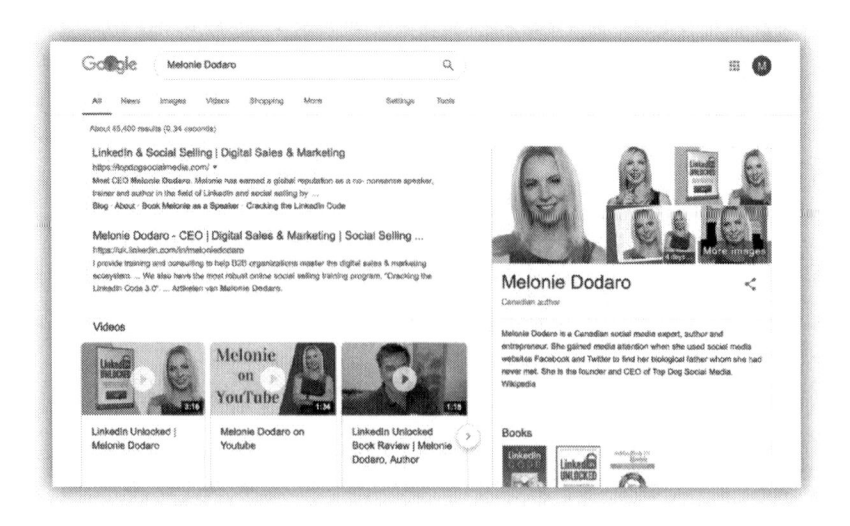

On the other hand, what if your search came up with nothing or almost nothing about you? This information (or lack of) can have a significant impact on your chances as a job candidate. Having an online presence has become critical in the modern world of work as most recruiters and hiring managers rely on online searches and social media when assessing potential employees. If you're not on the web, it's almost as if you don't exist. A standard resume and cover letter are no longer enough to get you an exceptional job.

It's likely you're already using social media. What is unlikely is that you use social media to help you get your dream job. You're probably more comfortable using social media sharing photos, liking your friends' posts, and replying to their comments than you are sharing your projects, connecting with other researchers in your subject matter, or engaging in conversations with experts in your field. This needs to change.

How LinkedIn Differs from Other Social Media Platforms

The good news is LinkedIn is not very different from other social media platforms—technically, structurally, and practically speaking. Setting up an account and using it shouldn't be a challenge for you. Now, for the harder news—there is no bad news, by the way! Are you ready?

Let's go back to the dinner etiquette class mentioned at the beginning of this section. Miguel remembers at the time feeling silly following all the rules of dining like a professional. That was until he started his first job in London and began attending business dinners and gala events, where he had a chance to put into practice his "silly" etiquette skills. On some occasions, a few people commented on his excellent table manners and showed him the same respect they showed older and more experienced professionals at the table. Even more surprising, often he felt he received more attention and admiration than others because the people at his table didn't expect someone as young and inexperienced as he was to have the confidence and the refined manners of a well-seasoned professional. The same can happen to you on LinkedIn if you pay attention to the small details and act as the professional nobody expected you to be.

> *"It takes 20 years to build a reputation and five minutes to ruin it. If you think about that, you'll do things differently."*
>
> – Warren Buffet

Now that you know the things you should do, let's talk about the things you should *never* do on LinkedIn. While much of this advice may seem obvious, you don't want to assume it will be second nature to you. Even the most successful professionals make mistakes that tarnish their reputations so severely that their careers and organizations suffer as a result. Luckily, you won't be answering to thousands of employees and shareholders just yet, but you *will* eventually have someone who really matters taking a close look at your actions on LinkedIn.

You shouldn't let the fear of making mistakes keep you from using LinkedIn effectively, but you should know what you need to avoid doing.

LinkedIn's Don'ts:

1. **Don't spam**: Please, don't be that person trying to connect with as many people as possible in the hopes that someone will eventually reply to you. No professional would ever do that, and you shouldn't either. At the very least, you will be consistently ignored; at worst,

3. **Engage and share intelligently**: Everything you engage with and share on social media is being judged. It forms an integral part of your online presence and reputation. While sharing an embarrassing photo or posting a rude comment can affect your friendship with someone, doing something similar on LinkedIn can cost you your job or worse. Engaging and sharing intelligently is about not only choosing appropriate content but also understanding the why, who, how, and what. This means having a clear objective, knowing your target audience, planning how you'd want to reach them, and deciding what content will resonate with them the most. Stay active and regularly share relevant content at least a few times a week.

4. **Nurture your network**: As you build your LinkedIn network, stay on top of your new relationships. You do this by finding ways and reasons to keep in touch with people. Birthdays, work anniversaries, and other celebrations—which you should add to your calendar—are all good reasons to drop a note to your new connection. You can also keep up to date with what your connections are sharing on LinkedIn by commenting on, liking, and sharing their content. This is incredibly important if you want to be memorable in the minds of those influencers and decision-makers who hold the key to your career success.

5. **Have confidence**: One of the most important things students and graduates need to do on LinkedIn is to act with confidence. Yes, we've used the word *acting* because at this point it doesn't matter if you're actually confident. You need to see yourself as a professional—not just as a student or graduate searching for a job. There is no reason for you to feel inferior or as if you need to beg for opportunities. You simply need to have the self-belief to create the most impressive profile among your peers, the determination to share unique content that matters to your professional relationships, and the confidence to approach anyone on LinkedIn who can help you achieve your goals… and we mean *anyone*. Get these things right, and you will find that LinkedIn is not only a useful but also an exciting place to spend your time, effort, and energy on.

Here it is: getting truly remarkable value from LinkedIn takes time, effort, and energy, unlike anything you've experienced with social media. This will not be the place for you to get instant gratification with a simple click or post something without much thought.

You will need to think of LinkedIn very differently from the way you think about Facebook, Twitter, Instagram, and other social sites. That's probably not a surprise, but it's still one of the things that prevent many students from using the platform at all.

You get on the platform, and suddenly you don't feel it makes sense, or you see a bunch of content that doesn't seem to relate to you. Guess what? Remember our discussion about blind spots in the last chapter? LinkedIn is one of those professional blind spots—the stuff you don't know you don't know.

The first thing you need to change is your mindset and expectations so that your inner narrative sounds like this:

LinkedIn is a tool I need to learn how to use to better understand and articulate what I'm passionate about so that I can develop my dream career. It's normal for it to feel unfamiliar, difficult to use, and overwhelming in the beginning, but that will not stop me from putting in the time, effort, and energy to use it effectively. I will do this because I know I can achieve incredible outcomes within the next few months and year, such as _____ and _____ _____, that would bring me closer to my dream career.

(Fill in the blanks with what you'd like to achieve after reading this book.)

LinkedIn will give you the ability to build an all-star professional profile that will showcase your best university work and achievements. It will also give you the ability to build relationships with people who can open doors for you as well as show you doors you didn't even know existed. You can find and share content that matters to your job market and transform your life and career in ways that no other social media platform currently can.

What to Do and What to Avoid

Have you ever taken a dinner etiquette class? When Miguel was at university, he took one with his pre-law fraternity. It was an hour-long mock dinner, teaching the attendees what the different plates and glasses mean; how to use different forks, spoons, and knives, depending on the food served; where to place your napkin; how to excuse yourself from the table; how to signal you've finished your meal; and even what direction you should pass things around the table. Thankfully, LinkedIn etiquette is not as prescriptive. However, it does warrant a few pages in this book.

LinkedIn Do's:

1. **Be authentic**: In other words, be yourself, but do it professionally. You don't need to open up about everything in your personal life, but it *is* important to feel comfortable sharing what makes you a unique candidate for the job you want. On the other hand, don't try to mimic what others are doing or try to pass for something you're not. We can't tell you how often we hear career advisors trying to coach students into acting, writing, and speaking like someone else so they can get hired for a job that doesn't fit them. Please, don't fall into this trap.

2. **Personalize your outreach**: Before you reach out to a stranger on LinkedIn, you must research them enough to personalize your connection request, message, or an InMail communication. This means knowing enough about the person and what they care about to write a meaningful note to them. The goal is to increase the likelihood of them accepting your connection request and replying to you. Getting this right as a student or young graduate is critical to ensure you're taken seriously since you will be depending on the goodwill of your network. Real professionals help others without always expecting something in return, but they still prefer to deal with other professionals who approach them respectfully and thoughtfully. Do your best to make sure that's you.

you'll gain a bad reputation that'll spread like wildfire. The same goes for messaging people at a company where you want to apply for a job. Be extra careful about how you approach these conversations as you never know who is talking to whom. I'm all for putting in the time and effort to get that interview, but don't get so desperate that you hurt your chances before you even start the race.

2. **Don't write essays**: Leave your academic writing style for your university work. Plain and simple, you do not need to prove your worth on LinkedIn by showcasing a broad vocabulary or using technical terms. Take a moment to observe how other professionals write on LinkedIn. You'll find that business writing is usually short, simple, and direct. If you can say it in fewer words, you should. Don't over analyze, either. Your tone on LinkedIn should be professional yet conversational. People will respect your ideas, thoughts, and opinions if they are well-written, relevant, and easy for anyone to understand. LinkedIn is full of busy professionals—don't waste their time, and get straight to the point.

3. **Don't be too private or selective**: At some point, you'll be fine-tuning your privacy settings on LinkedIn. As a student or recent graduate, you should follow a straightforward approach: stay open. While it might make sense to protect yourself on social media sites such as Facebook, on LinkedIn your goal is to build relationships with professionals. This won't happen if you make it difficult for people to find and connect with you. You should be comfortable with the information you share on LinkedIn, allowing everyone to see it. That's the point of joining a professional network.

4. **Don't limit yourself to only a few types of professionals when connecting or accepting connections:** Just because you're interested in working for a pharmaceutical company doesn't mean you should connect only with pharmaceutical professionals. You never know where opportunities will come from, so don't be picky. Once you're more established in your career, you can be more selective.

5. **Don't plagiarize**: This advice should sound familiar to you: trying to pass the work of others as your own is among the worst things

you could do on LinkedIn. You shouldn't do it as a student, and you certainly shouldn't do it as a professional. These days, finding and sharing content is effortless. You still need to identify the original source of the information and give credit to its creator. Citing your sources is especially important when publishing your own articles on LinkedIn, which we will cover in a later chapter.

6. **Don't be slow to respond**: Caveat: fast response doesn't mean thoughtless—always put thought into everything you do on LinkedIn. But don't take too long to engage with and reply to the members of your network. If someone has taken the time to connect with you, be sure to thank them. If someone has sent you a thoughtful message, try to respond within 24 hours. If someone has commented on or shared your LinkedIn post, be sure to respond in kind. You get the picture. Don't keep your network waiting. Suspense and drama don't work well for professionals on LinkedIn.

As you spend more time on LinkedIn, you'll see the etiquette and best practices most professionals follow. Unfortunately, you'll also come across some very poor examples of LinkedIn behavior. Those stand out more on LinkedIn than they do on other social media platforms. As a student or graduate, take seriously the information in this chapter so you stand out only for the right reasons.

Things to focus on in the next seven days:

1. Understand the best practices of using LinkedIn effectively.
2. Remind yourself of what you should avoid doing on LinkedIn.
3. Decide what you want to be known for on LinkedIn 3-12 months from now.

Things to do in the next seven days:

1. Write down the small and big wins you'd like to achieve with LinkedIn.
2. Share your LinkedIn goals with your friends and loved ones.
3. Start engaging with people and content on LinkedIn—like, comment, reply, share, etc.

CHAPTER 5

DETERMINE YOUR TARGET AUDIENCE AND IDEAL EMPLOYERS

Everything you do on LinkedIn should be for *someone* and *something* specific to your career needs. Whether you're building your profile, choosing what skills and experience to showcase, or deciding what to share on LinkedIn, you need to think of your target audience and ideal employers. Whom you need to speak to and why should they listen to you is what we cover in this chapter.

Most students don't consider the target audience of their profiles when starting on LinkedIn. Many don't focus on industries and roles relevant to the job market of today and the future, or they restrict themselves to their current fields of studies without concentrating on a broader range of skills and experience necessary to address the demands of the modern job market. Remember that LinkedIn is your chance to go wide when it comes to attracting the right influencers and decision-makers.

Identify Influencers Who Matter to You

We used the word *influencers* several times in the last few chapters—with good reason. In every region, industry, and company, some professionals stand out for being exceptional at what they do. This doesn't mean they're rich and famous, but it does usually mean they are well-respected experts with many followers because of the unique value they offer.

They can be published authors, TED speakers, entrepreneurs, bloggers, artists, journalists, executives, or speakers at large conferences. You should keep your eye out for these people because they usually have something important to say about thinking, working, and living in new and better ways. Isn't that what you're also trying to accomplish?

To identify the influencers who matter to your career, start by searching for top influencers on LinkedIn. You'll find a list of "top voices" featuring some of the most widely recognized writers on a range of topics who publish on LinkedIn. If you do a Google search, you'll also come up with a variety of articles about top influencers you should follow regardless of industries.

This is an excellent place to start to get an idea of why these people are influencers, how they became influencers, and what particular influence they have. Are they known for productivity tips, wellbeing best practices, life hacks, or career advice? What can you learn from them and apply to your life and work that can set you apart from other job candidates?

Learning from influencers will also give you an unprecedented look at what actually matters to people, companies, and industries in your chosen career both today and in the future. You'll read about the most significant challenges they're dealing with as well as the biggest opportunities they're preparing for.

Where do you fit in? Being able to engage in conversations on these topics means you go from being just a student to a sophisticated professional in your field. It really does pay to learn from influencers, and if you ever get in touch with them, you might create the opportunity of a lifetime. That's why this book exists!

How to Find the Right People in Companies

Next, look for companies employing people already working in your ideal career. It's okay if you don't yet know what that career looks like. Just start by writing down a list of departments, functions, and job titles aligned with your passions, your natural skills and abilities, and the current and future demands of the job market.

For example, if you're studying communications or journalism and passionate about and skilled at writing, you could look for people in marketing, internal communications, creative writing, and news editing. Don't worry about specific industries and companies for now as you'll want to keep your search broad to get exposure to as many different types of professionals as possible.

You might notice there aren't many jobs at your local newspaper or news channel, but you might come to realize many smart and creative people like you are working at fast-growing startups in your region. A closer look might reveal you are more likely to get a good entry-level job at a smaller company than a large corporation, doing what you love. Exploring LinkedIn profiles of employees of smaller companies, you might also notice they tend to be happier and stay longer in their jobs than employees of larger organizations.

The example above is meant to show you how finding the right people in companies can change your whole perspective on what's possible for your own career success. Your personal experiences could be similar to or vastly different from those of other people, but in all cases, you should be discovering and learning about new opportunities you might have not known about before. That's how you'll know you're finding the right people and on your way to understanding what matters to them.

Criteria for Finding Companies That Invest in Their Employees

As you research people on LinkedIn, take note of where they work and what they do. Your own research on LinkedIn can reveal much more about the kind of people a company hires than the company's videos, websites, and job descriptions can.

For example, you could research a company by looking through its employees' profile photos, headlines, and summaries. Do the professionals in that company look and sound like colleagues you would enjoy working with? Pay particular attention to their summaries, which should be well-written and cover what they're passionate about.

Next, Miguel shares the benefits of learning how to use LinkedIn for company research based on his own experience.

"When I did this research, I began to see patterns in the way employees at specific companies designed and organized their profiles. I remember one particular company where male employees wore similar suits with white shirts and red ties. Seriously! For me, that was over the top, and I would never be able to work for any organization that dictated or strongly recommended how I should dress or what color scheme I should wear for my LinkedIn profile picture. I would never fit in any company like that.

In another example, I researched a company where employees either had no profile pictures or badly outdated or poor-quality pictures. I later discovered employees at this company were fearful of using social media. They were discouraged to share anything they did at work online. Some companies might have an entirely legitimate reason for being so careful (e.g., financial or professional services), but knowing how much I thrive on sharing my work and networking online, I knew that any workplace culture that would prevent me from doing this would be too stifling for me.

The question is, what's important to *you*?

I'll admit, I never had a solid plan or criteria when I first started using LinkedIn. It was through several years of trial and error that I naturally learned and developed better ways to make career decisions. Those small details I noticed in profiles and company pages began to make more sense when I met people offline and spent time at their offices. My hope is you'll be grasping this much quicker than I did by reading this chapter and applying its lessons!"

Company Mission and Values

Here's a list of Miguel's ten criteria when assessing a company, prioritized by what matters most to him:

1. Vision, mission, and values
2. Culture
3. People and leaders

Determine Your Target Audience and Ideal Employers

4. Influence, reputation, and credibility
5. Salary, benefits, and other rewards
6. Career growth
7. Products and services
8. Types of jobs
9. Skills and experience gained
10. Location and commute

When he researches a company or a job, one of the first things he does is he watches the company's videos describing its vision, mission, and values. Its vision statement should tell you why it exists and how it plans to achieve its goals. Its mission statement should explain what it does and whom it does it for, broadly covering the value it offers its customers. Its values statement should highlight its expectations around behaviors and actions that guide the way work is done at the company.

As a student, you should think carefully about your own personal vision, mission, and values and how closely they align with the organizations you want to work for.

Workplace Culture and Expectations

The environment of a workplace and the wellbeing of its employees are tied to company culture. You may hear of company cultures that promote creativity, inclusiveness, and diversity or of those that promote aggressive competitiveness, creating stressful work environments.

On LinkedIn, you'll notice company pages that list a section called "Life" that dives into the culture of the organization. Reading through this section will give you a window into what the company stands for and cares about. You might learn about industry leaders who work there, news or recent announcements about the company, philanthropy projects, and examples of community engagement.

Pay close attention to what you see there because it will be the best way to assess what it might feel like to work in the company until you speak to or meet someone from that organization. Then, you can judge whether your assumptions still stand. You don't want to work anywhere you can't be yourself.

Gather Information on the People Who Matter

You'll spend much time working with people doing other jobs in your chosen career. Look at employee profiles representing different parts of the business and not just the one you're interested in. Do the same for senior leaders. Prepare questions to ask, and reach out to several employees on LinkedIn.

In the next section of this book, we explore some of the most effective ways to reach out to people via LinkedIn so you can get helpful responses. By connecting on LinkedIn, you'll be able to schedule calls and meetings with these employees and gain firsthand impressions about their attitudes toward the company: whether they seem happy, indifferent or unhappy to be there.

Your direct communication with employees can also reveal how hard people work at the company and whether they play just as hard. Asking people of various age groups about it will give you the best perspective on the work-life balance.

Also consider the company's influence, reputation, and credibility. At the start and end of every day, will you be proud to work at that company? Will you be proud of the work you do? Does the company have a good influence on the world; does it have a positive reputation; and do people consider it to be credible?

Once you decide to work for a company, you also choose to represent that company. Who the people in the company are and what they do is now part of who you are and what you do. You'd better feel comfortable and confident about your workplace because you will be judged by it throughout your life and career.

Research Companies Beyond the Basics

You want to make sure you are fairly compensated for the time, energy, and effort you put into your work. It should be aligned with your goals, lifestyle, skills, education, and experience. As a student or recent graduate, you will need to be realistic but also bold when researching opportunities, applying for jobs, and attending interviews.

What do entry-level jobs pay in your industry? What regions or cities have the highest salaries? Which companies have the best employee benefits? Are there any other rewards involved, like a commission or yearly bonus, that you need to consider on top of the base salary?

These days, it's much easier to get this information thanks to sites such as Glassdoor and LinkedIn. You can also access government websites covering an extensive range of professions with details on requirements and salaries.

One of Miguel's proudest moments early in his career was being promoted from an Associate to Customer Success Manager. With that, came new opportunities to work with larger, more strategic clients, more international travel to visit clients face-to-face, and a significant salary boost that allowed him to live without roommates. Since then, he is always thinking about career growth. Plenty of his friends feel their careers have stagnated. Although they're doing well and working hard, it seems as if something always gets in the way of them getting the promised promotion.

As you do your own research, make sure career growth is on your list. You might be excited just to get your first job, but a time will come when you'll be ready to advance. That's why it's important to work for a company that will support your learning and invest in your professional growth in return for the valuable work you do for them. Use LinkedIn to see the average tenure of employees at the company and how often they get promoted or move to new roles within the company.

In his book *The Alliance*[12], Reid Hoffman describes a new way to see the employer-employee relationship, reflecting the changes taking place in today's business environment. We should start seeing our team members and leaders as allies, willing to support our success. The company's sentiment toward its employees then should be: "If you help us have happy customers and grow the business, we'll help you learn and develop so you can advance your career."

---

12 Reid Hoffman, Ben Casnocha, Chris Yeh, *The Alliance: Managing Talent in the Networked Age,* (Boston: Harvard Business Review Press, 2014)

If you look closely and listen carefully, you'll begin to see and feel whether an employer trusts their employees. Do they provide opportunities for their employees to develop their careers, or are they fearful of their employees leaving the company?

Another question to ask yourself is, do you believe in and would you be proud to use the company's services and products? The answer reflects the company's influence, reputation, and credibility—a topic already discussed above. In this case, however, you want to look specifically at what the company makes and the value it offers its customers. What do customers say about its products and services? Check as many different sources of reviews as you can, and even consider asking some customers what they think about the company. Research employees working in product, marketing, or sales roles, and see how they represent the products and services of their company. In many cases, you'll be spending a lot of time using and promoting your company's product, so make sure you understand and believe in it.

We also suggest looking into the financial health of the company to see whether they're profitable, growing, or losing money. You can find this information easily for larger companies, often in the press or their annual reports. For smaller companies and startups, you may have to ask others for more information. You can also check whether the company received any funding—it's usually public information. No trustworthy employer should be deceptive about their company's financial health, but keep in mind they'll probably withhold specific numbers and information if they haven't hired you yet. Still, check their state of affairs the best you can so you're not joining a company struggling to pay their employees.

As you continue to do your employment research, keep your options open by looking at a variety of job types. Many times, the title or description of a job doesn't do it justice, and you need to dig deeper to really understand whether it'd be a good fit.

Looking at other open positions, you can get insights into the types of jobs the company is filling and whether it is growing in a particular area. Look at its recent hires, and see if you can spot anything that might help you understand why these people were successful at getting their jobs.

You should also compare the way the company promotes its jobs, including the language it uses, with that of other companies advertising similar roles. Even slight differences can influence your career decisions.

Every job requires specific skills and level of experience. A word of advice: don't ever let your lack of experience discourage you. The best jobs will not be advertised as student- or graduate-friendly. Many will ask for specific qualifications, industry focus, and years of experience. But unless the ad spells out such requirements explicitly, you don't need to consider them must-haves.

Look for words such as *similar* or *transferable* in a job advertisement. Such wording gives you the opportunity to showcase your unique value even if it doesn't quite fit the advertiser's expectations. Even if the ad doesn't have such wording, you should still apply, emphasizing your strength and suitability for the job. You have nothing to lose, and you'll be able to learn from rejections. It's better to get multiple rejections for the jobs you really want, finally landing one of them, than getting hired quickly for something you don't want. The latter can lead you down the slippery slope of an unfulfilled career, while the former can set you up for a successful career even if you have a long way to climb.

Last, but certainly not least, on the list of employment considerations is the job's location and the commute required. You don't want to say no to a job because of a 45-minute commute, but you probably don't want a position that will consume hours every day to get to and from either. You might be willing to make that sacrifice for your dream job, but in our experience, a long commute will eventually make you feel tired, frustrated, and uninspired. Research increasingly shows the damage a miserable commute can have on your life. What job would be worth so much that you'd sacrifice your health and/or family for?

To highlight the point, Miguel recalls one of his early employment experiences.

"One of my first jobs required that I catch the Central Line in the London Underground. Some mornings, I would have to let three or four trains pass by before there was enough space to jump in. Then I would travel for 40 minutes in crammed train carriages with the bags and armpits of grumpy commuters shoved in my face. I did that for about a year before I called it quits and made the necessary changes to my life and career."

Make sure you love the city where you work and have at least a bearable commute that doesn't leave you tired and upset. It all adds up, and it can either strengthen your work or take a tremendous toll on your life and happiness.

We hope this list has given you a good idea of what you need to consider to choose your ideal employer. Yours might look very different as you prioritize some things over others, but make sure you don't sacrifice any of the essentials that keep you healthy, happy, and productive. You'll gain the respect of prospective employers when they see your efforts to make sure the job is the best fit for you *and* for them.

Things to focus on in the next seven days:

1. Who makes and influences hiring decisions for the jobs you want to apply for?
2. In what ways do you expect your future employer to help you develop?
3. What kinds of products and solutions would you be most happy and proud to work with?

Things to do in the next seven days:

1. Make a list of the top five people to get to know for each job you apply for.
2. Research employee reviews for every company you're considering, paying attention to the best and the worst ones equally.
3. List your top 10 criteria of what matters most to you when choosing a job.

PART II:
YOUR PATH TO CAREER DEVELOPMENT ON LINKEDIN

CHAPTER 6

DESIGN YOUR LINKEDIN PROFILE

Every good designer knows that the success of their work depends largely on how people interpret and use their designs. You wouldn't start working on something without thinking about the kind of people you're creating your design for, right? Who are they? What do they care about? How will this make them feel? These are the kinds of questions you need to think about as you prepare to design your LinkedIn profile.

There is real art to designing one's profile, and you can see it in the profiles of the best and most successful professionals. They balance their unique voices with the needs of their audiences. While many professionals end up with cookie cutter profiles, sounding alike and speaking to no one in particular, a brilliantly designed profile stands out from the crowd because it elicits positive emotions about the owner of that profile and in the process makes the reader feel good about themselves.

One of the most significant objections to creating a LinkedIn profile students and graduates often present is they don't know what belongs on their LinkedIn profiles.

If we look more closely at their reasons, they hesitate because they are:

- unsure whether what they care about will be valued by the LinkedIn audience

- afraid that some of their interests, skills, and experiences don't align with their fields of studies
- worried about being judged because they are students or recent graduates without much work experience
- confused about how to use LinkedIn in a way that satisfies and benefits them quickly
- resistant to using social media in a professional context because it feels risky, unfamiliar, and time-consuming.

Guess what? Even professionals with many years of experience face many of the same problems. It's one of the main reasons many weak or incomplete profiles exist on LinkedIn, telling you very little about the people behind them. While some professionals can get away without having brilliant LinkedIn profiles because of their offline reputations and the value they offer, most people need to have a great LinkedIn profile to advance their careers.

To make your LinkedIn profile work for you, you need to:

- Showcase what you're genuinely passionate about that could potentially lead to your ideal career, no matter how ridiculous or far-fetched you think it sounds to others. Someone out there may be desperately looking for that fire that most candidates lack.
- Be comfortable showing how dynamic you are by having a range of different interests, skills, and experiences. That unique combination could make you the ideal candidate for a fantastic opportunity without the need for you to be the smartest, loudest, or best-looking candidate.
- Know that being a student or recent graduate without much work experience could be to your advantage. You can prove your value in other unique and surprising ways that will help you stand out from the crowd, especially if your LinkedIn profile and activity look and sound a lot better than those of more experienced candidates.

- Stop yourself from expecting instant gratification on LinkedIn the way you expect it on other social media platforms. If you're not getting the results you want, it's time to tweak your approach.

Who you are on LinkedIn and other social media sites is starting to matter just as much as who you are offline. That's because companies searching for talent seek out online information about the candidates. That means when assessing your suitability for a job, they will be looking at your online presence and reputation. A Google search of your name might list your LinkedIn profile on the first page of search results.

Remember that even the most qualified people may be overlooked because of their poor online presence. Since you can't influence decision-makers directly, the only way you can help yourself is by managing your own online presence. You want recruiters to skip you for the right reasons—not because they can't find you, need more information about you, or don't appreciate that you're sharing controversial or inflammatory views on LinkedIn.

At the same time, you don't want to pretend to be someone else online so that you can get approached by recruiters and secure interviews from as many companies as possible. Trying to cater to everyone on LinkedIn may get you some attention, but chances are it won't land you your dream job.

Remember that people will be expecting to meet the person they see on that LinkedIn profile, and if your online persona doesn't match the real you, your credibility is at risk, which is exactly what you want to avoid at all costs in your interviews! What is the least damaging thing that can happen in this situation? You don't get the job and move on. The worst? You get the job because of your deception and make a long and miserable career out of it. We are confident you don't want that.

Stand Out on LinkedIn from Day One

We hope by now you've realized you don't need to be an expert to look amazing on LinkedIn from day one. The key is knowing why you're using it and what your target audience is—the people who will bring you closer to your ideal career.

It might be easy for you to start copying and pasting parts of your resume into your LinkedIn profile. While some of that information may be relevant, we don't recommend you do this. This won't help you stand out when a recruiter gets your resume that looks exactly as your LinkedIn profile.

Here are a few other reasons why you don't want to use your resume as a substitute for your LinkedIn profile:

- it's way too easy and doesn't require you to think or consider an original approach to showcasing your interests, skills, and experience
- it may include phrases, words, abbreviations, and acronyms that wouldn't resonate with your ideal audience on LinkedIn
- the formatting of your resume may over-simplify valuable information, preventing you from showcasing your work and achievements.

Designing an attractive LinkedIn profile doesn't mean starting from scratch. But it requires you to share something unique about yourself, such as a story. If you already have a LinkedIn profile, you still want to look closely at every aspect of it and think carefully about what you have and don't have there. If you don't feel ready to update your profile, as you critically assess it, write down your thoughts for future changes.

Again, to ensure you nail your LinkedIn profile, ask yourself: *Does my profile really represent who I am and whom I want to become?*

If we were to use one word to describe the most important aspect of your profile, it would be *authenticity*. You need to show that while you may not be in the big leagues yet, you're already looking and behaving as if you were. Is there any part of your profile that doesn't accurately describe you? Does your profile sound like it could be describing any other student or graduate you know?

The next thing you should ask yourself is: *Does my profile sound mostly like I'm a student, an aspiring graduate, or a professional with a lot of value to offer?*

We've talked about the importance of students becoming sought-after professionals before they graduate. This strategy includes your LinkedIn profile. When they first start using LinkedIn, many students feel as if they need to feature the fact that they're students in a specific university or program in their headline or About section. The fact that you're a student today should *not* be the focus of your profile. You already have an education section where you can list your student, degree, and university details. What you *should* highlight prominently is your passion, interests, skills, and experience above and beyond your student life and degree plan. We're not saying conceal the fact you're in school—just don't put up a billboard with the word *student* on it and not much else.

The best profiles tell a story eliciting an emotional response that aligns with the vision, mission, and culture of an organization. It makes a candidate likable, valuable, and memorable.

The Essentials of Your LinkedIn Profile

By essentials, we mean all the parts of your profile you should complete if you want to have a good foundation for your professional brand. We explain each of the sections and their purpose next.

1. **Photo and Background Image**: Your photo and background image are the first things people see when they land on your profile. Choose a photo that accurately and professionally portrays who you are. The same thing applies to your background image. Choose one that is high quality, doesn't look awkwardly cropped, and isn't too distracting (ideal size is 1536 x 768 pixels). Landscapes, cityscapes, and other natural settings work well for the larger background photo that acts as a banner at the top of your profile. You can discretely update these images without notifying others in your network.

2. **Headline**: This is the first thing people read when they come across your profile in search results or when viewing the full version of your profile. By default, it displays your current job title and company. Update this section so it tells the reader what you're passionate about and the unique value you offer to others. It can read as a short statement. Also consider the keywords you'd like to include in that headline. For example, if your ideal career is in cyber security, choose

one or a few relevant keywords. The keywords increase the likelihood that your profile will come up in the right search results for your target audience. Get creative with it, and let your personality come through so it doesn't sound like a description of every other student or professional.

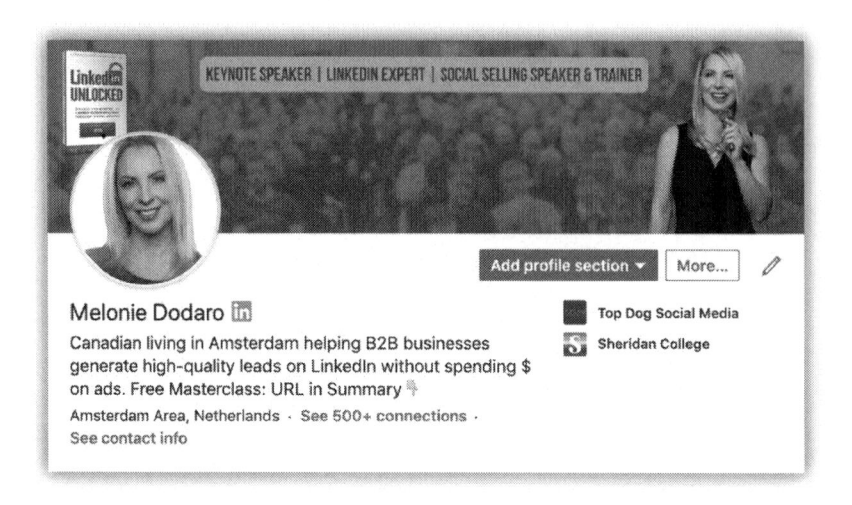

![Melonie Dodaro LinkedIn profile screenshot showing banner "KEYNOTE SPEAKER | LINKEDIN EXPERT | SOCIAL SELLING SPEAKER & TRAINER", profile photo, and headline: "Canadian living in Amsterdam helping B2B businesses generate high-quality leads on LinkedIn without spending $ on ads. Free Masterclass: URL in Summary". Location: Amsterdam Area, Netherlands · See 500+ connections. Experience: Top Dog Social Media, Sheridan College.]

3. **About (formerly Summary)**: This is the most crucial part of your profile, especially if you don't have a lot of work experience, endorsements, and recommendations to highlight your skills and reputation. The About section is an opportunity to tell your story. This will require you to take your time and think carefully about what parts of your personal experience matter the most in highlighting your personality, character, values, accomplishments, and ambitions. It should be written in the first-person voice, using a conversational tone. Structure it as you would the answer to the question "Can you tell me about yourself?" Remember, you can use keywords here too, so make sure you understand what matters in your ideal career today and tomorrow to include the right ones. You can start by getting inspiration from others' About sections.

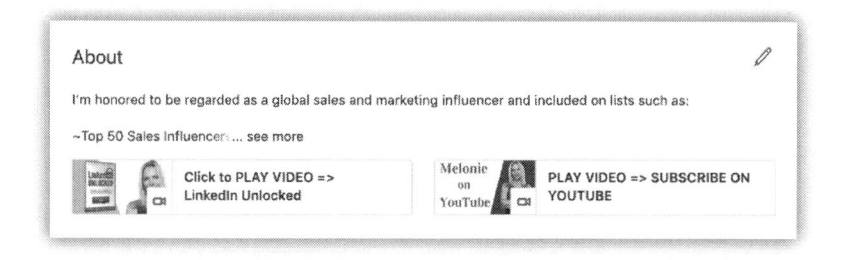

4. **Work Experience**: This might seem like a problematic section of your profile if you haven't held any formal jobs, but you can think about your work experience in a number of ways. Think about any past short-term work where you learned something new and gained transferable skills. This includes working in the family business, being an office assistant, organizing an event, running a campaign, or holding a position as part of a student organization. Make sure you provide details about your role and responsibilities and any unique contributions you made. It's even better if these are measurable improvements, highlighting your potential to think analytically and deliver strong results. We highly recommend not leaving this section blank.

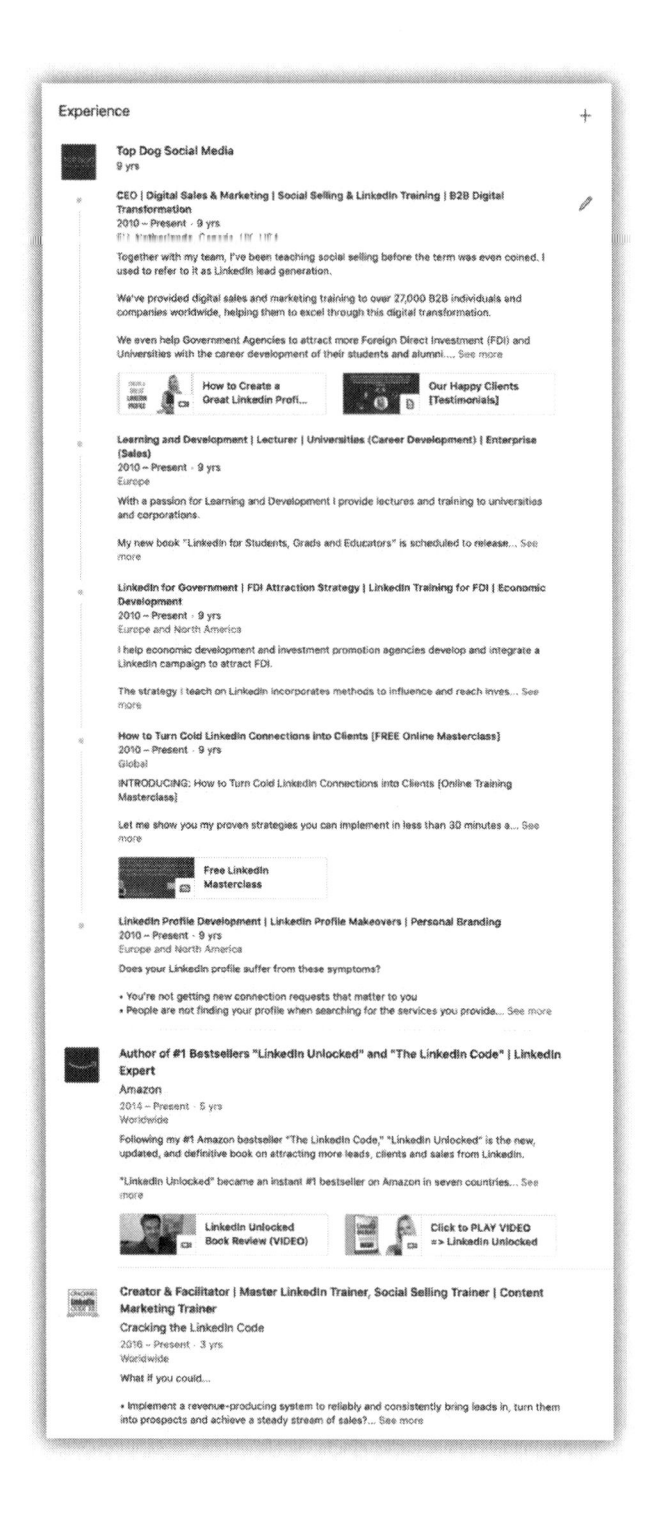

LinkedIn For Students, Graduates, and Educators

5. **Education**: This section should be straightforward, but we still encounter many student and graduate profiles that merely list the names of universities and degrees. Surely there is much more you can share with your professional network about your education, right? Include any unique coursework you've done that promotes your specialization in a particular field or your broad range of experience in different subjects. If you'd like to highlight any research you've done for lab work, essays, or dissertations, this is the place to do it as well. You should also think of any online courses or other learning experiences outside your school that could promote your dedication to what you're passionate about even further. In today's job market, you will continuously need to learn to stay relevant and advance in your career. Demonstrate you understand that in this section.

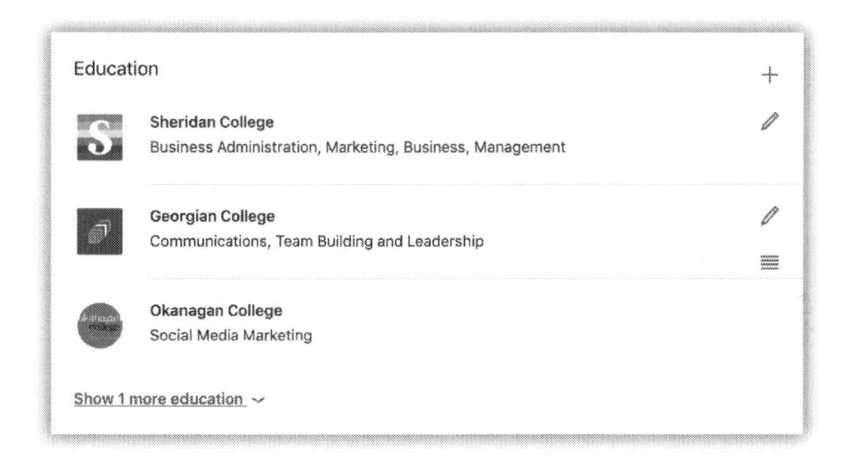

```
Education                                                    +

    Sheridan College                                         ✏
    Business Administration, Marketing, Business, Management

    Georgian College                                         ✏
    Communications, Team Building and Leadership

    Okanagan College
    Social Media Marketing

Show 1 more education ⌄
```

6. **Skills and Endorsements**: This section of your profile allows those who know you to tell the world what you are good at. To take advantage of this section, make a list of all the different skills you believe you already possess. Remember, you don't have to be an expert. These are the skills you've used in the past—whether it's your paid or volunteer work, student life or academic endeavors. For inspiration, look at the profiles of the professionals in your chosen field to see what kinds of skills they've included. When you add new skills,

see if you can find people who witnessed you using them, and then ask those people to endorse those skills. For example, if a faculty member observed you presenting in class and you did well on that assignment, ask that person to endorse your public speaking skills. Think of all those classes, assignments, and projects you've done that could lead to even more endorsements!

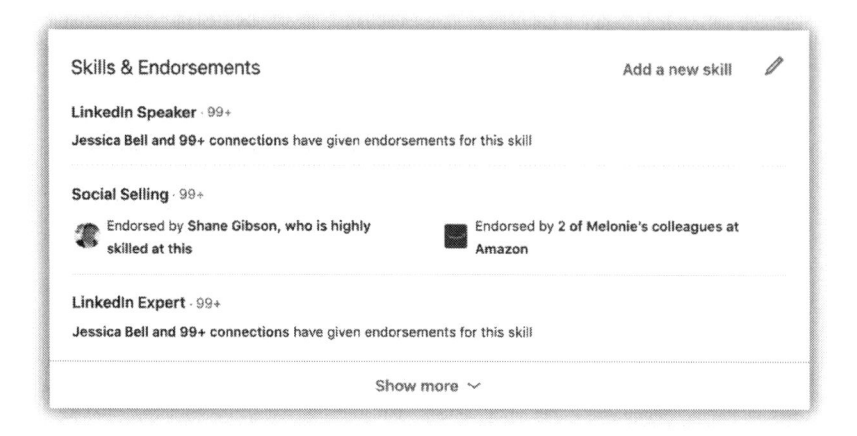

```
Skills & Endorsements                                    Add a new skill  ✏

LinkedIn Speaker · 99+
Jessica Bell and 99+ connections have given endorsements for this skill

Social Selling · 99+
    Endorsed by Shane Gibson, who is highly        Endorsed by 2 of Melonie's colleagues at
    skilled at this                                 Amazon

LinkedIn Expert · 99+
Jessica Bell and 99+ connections have given endorsements for this skill

                        Show more  ⌄
```

7. **Recommendations**: Getting recommended by others on LinkedIn is a fantastic way to make yourself even more valuable and marketable. Professional recommendations aren't given lightly, and they do require effort on both sides to make them happen. You need to think carefully about whom you ask. It can't be just anyone as you want to make sure you choose people who have seen your work and can genuinely speak about your unique contributions. It's even better if they are influential and well-respected. When asking for recommendations, we suggest crafting a message that is brief and direct. Tell the recommender explicitly what you would like to be recommended for so that it's much easier for them to write the recommendation you need.

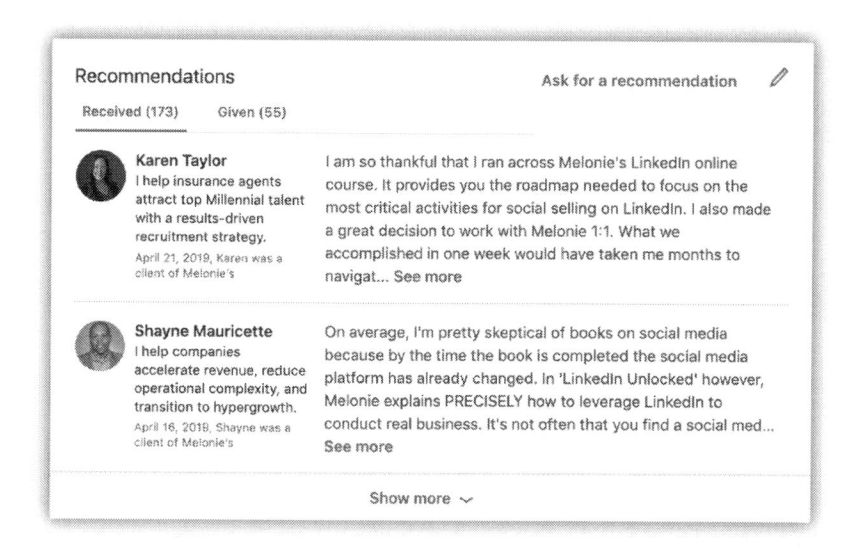

> **Recommendations**　　　　　　　　　　　Ask for a recommendation
>
> Received (173)　　Given (55)
>
> **Karen Taylor**
> I help insurance agents attract top Millennial talent with a results-driven recruitment strategy.
> April 21, 2019, Karen was a client of Melonie's
>
> I am so thankful that I ran across Melonie's LinkedIn online course. It provides you the roadmap needed to focus on the most critical activities for social selling on LinkedIn. I also made a great decision to work with Melonie 1:1. What we accomplished in one week would have taken me months to navigat... See more
>
> **Shayne Mauricette**
> I help companies accelerate revenue, reduce operational complexity, and transition to hypergrowth.
> April 16, 2018, Shayne was a client of Melonie's
>
> On average, I'm pretty skeptical of books on social media because by the time the book is completed the social media platform has already changed. In 'LinkedIn Unlocked' however, Melonie explains PRECISELY how to leverage LinkedIn to conduct real business. It's not often that you find a social med... See more
>
> Show more ⌄

8. **Volunteer Experience**: Whether you're still at university or have already graduated, you have likely volunteered in some way throughout your student life. If you haven't, we recommend you start looking for as many opportunities as possible. This is especially important if you're not planning on working anytime soon and won't have much work experience to list on your profile. Support causes you feel strongly about, and find ways to give back to your community. A simple search online or discussion with staff and faculty will help you uncover volunteering opportunities. Every great employer wants to hear about what you've done for others in any capacity.

> **Volunteer Experience**
>
> **Committee Chair of Social Media | Board of Director | Social Media Advisor**
> Conservative Party of Canada
> 2011 – 2014 • 3 yrs
> Politics
>
> Served on the Board of Directors and as Committee Chair of Social Media for the Conservative Party of Canada.
>
> Was the Social Media Advisor to Member of Parliament (MP) Ron Cannan.
>
> **Advisor for Internet Marketing Program**
> Centre for Arts and Technology
> 2012 • less than a year
> Education
>
> I was an advisor in helping to create the curriculum for the new Internet Marketing program that was being offered to students at the Centre of Arts & Technology in Canada.

Now, you might be thinking you couldn't put all this information on your profile in one day. While we agree it's not easy, it's possible. Thanks to having a network of over half a billion members and a multitude of different ways to connect and message others, you can start seeing results quickly when you put in the time and effort to design your profile. The more complete it is, the more likely you'll attract the right people.

Bringing Your Professional Brand to Life

In this last section, we show you how to enhance your LinkedIn profile so it represents you as a true professional. We revisit some of the sections discussed in the last few pages, describing best practices that will help you bring your professional brand to life.

Most importantly, we look at the style and type of content that can help you stand out for the right reasons and attract your ideal employers. It's time for you to go above and beyond what you've done so far with your profile essentials and start seeing your profile as a dynamic and continuously evolving canvas that draws the viewer into an experience. A static page can never do that. It's time for your creativity to flourish!

What do you want your photo to represent?

We know your photo depends on your personal style, but consider the following critical points.

Firstly, remember that looking your best does not mean you need to wear formal business attire. If you were interviewing for a job or meeting a new customer, what would you wear? That's what we should see you wearing in your photo.

Secondly, consider your body language. Make sure your pose doesn't look forced or unnatural. When posing, go for confidence—look directly into the camera with a relaxed smile and good body posture while projecting a welcoming vibe.

Finally, think about location and environment. Make sure you choose a place where you're not distracted and feel completely comfortable. Also, make sure the background of your photograph is appropriate for the professional network. Remember to update your photo every couple of years or more frequently if your style and appearance changed significantly. Your picture should represent who you are in a real business setting. Don't overdo it! Make it easy for people to put a name to your face.

What's the most compelling thing about you?

If you could tell only one story to highlight who you are, what would it be? It's probably not an easy question to answer, but we want you to think about it because your LinkedIn profile should tell us something about you we can't find anywhere else. That unique bit of information belongs in your About section. Thousands of other people could have the same combination of degree, interests, skills, and ambitions as you do. However, you may be the only person with a unique blend of particular experiences that will set you apart from everyone else. What will make you memorable?

What inspires and motivates you in life?

Think about the last thing you saw, read, or heard that motivated you to take action. Was it a book, video, article, image, quote, or podcast? Share this content in the Media section of your profile. Tell us why it matters to you and what it motivates you to do. Do the same thing for your Experience section, where you can also add media content. If you've interned or worked anywhere, add content that tells the reader of your profile something interesting about the organization, its products and services, and the role you had while you were there. Typically, you can find most of this information on a company's website or blog, if there is one. Here, you can add anything you worked on that can be shared publicly, like a presentation or marketing campaign.

Show us who you are, don't just tell us.

What to focus on in the next seven days:

1. Whom do you want to attract to your LinkedIn profile?
2. What's your story? What makes you special and memorable?
3. Consider the experiences you've had so you can complete all the essential sections of your LinkedIn profile.

What to start doing in the next seven days:

1. Describe your ideal LinkedIn audience in as much detail as possible: who they are, what they care about, and why they would be looking for someone like you.
2. Write your LinkedIn headline and About section, then share it with those you respect to get their feedback.
3. Choose or take a photo for your LinkedIn profile. Remember, this is the professional look you want to have when attending interviews.

CHAPTER 7

BUILD RELATIONSHIPS AND OPEN DOORS

Build Strong Relationships with the Right People

Now we're really getting to the lifeblood of your career development success on LinkedIn. Nothing will determine how successful you are using LinkedIn more than the connections and relationships you build there.

Think about some of the most rewarding moments of your life. We bet most of them include people you care about, such as family, friends, and co-workers. Throughout our lives, we nurture these relationships because they give us something meaningful in return, whether that's love, friendship, or better career opportunities. They matter to us because we matter to them.

LinkedIn is not very different in this regard. It's all about forming relationships with the right people. The question is, how do you know who the right people are?

What stands between you and your ideal career is a bunch of locked doors, all requiring different keys to open them. Some will be obvious, while others will be partially hidden. Most will not be visible to you. The right people can open these doors for you if they feel they know, like, and trust you.

LinkedIn supercharges the relationship-building process by making it super easy for you to find professionals you can learn from. First, think about the best approach to make new connections within a particular industry and company. Next, decide on the target number of new connections you will make each week or month. At this point, keep an open mind about the people who can offer you insights and other opportunities, and cast a wide net. Sometimes it takes only one great relationship to open a door that would have otherwise remained closed or never discovered.

If you feel hesitant to approach people you don't know, you are not alone. Many students and graduates have the same concern. It becomes an even bigger problem when it involves networking with professionals. For whatever reason, many of our schools and universities don't require or encourage their students to branch out and build relationships with employers and organizations in their communities by integrating such an outreach in their curricula, not just in one course or module. Because of that, students don't learn critical soft skills necessary for their success after graduation. If you can relate, you've picked up the right book because we're about to tell you how easy and effective relationship-building can be when you're using LinkedIn.

If you still feel skeptical about using LinkedIn to help you find your next career step, consider reading an article called "How a Simple LinkedIn Message That Took 2 Minutes to Write Landed Me My Dream Job".[13] The article shows the incredible power of taking the non-traditional route of getting the attention of employers and building relationships with them. You'll see that small actions on LinkedIn can make all the difference when you (a) spend time understanding the people who make hiring decisions, (b) use your network to find the best way in, and (c) demonstrate how your skills match the job you are after.

If you're not sure how you would ever get to this point, keep reading. The next chapters will show you how you can make this happen!

Network Within Your University and with Alumni

One of the best and easiest ways to start building relationships on LinkedIn is to look at the students, faculty, and staff at your university. Depending on

---

13 Elliott Bell, "How a Simple LinkedIn Message That Took 2 Minutes to Write Landed Me My Dream Job," *The Muse*, https://www.themuse.com/advice/how-a-simple-linkedin-message-that-took-2-minutes-to-write-landed-me-my-dream-job

the size of your school, you'll have the chance to connect with hundreds or thousands of individuals already on LinkedIn—if they're not, do everyone a favor and invite them!

Review your courses, university groups, social media channels, and university directories to find people you already know. You could have met them in a class, at an event, or in a study group. Your next step is to send them personalized LinkedIn connection requests.

Many professionals are conscientious and selective about whom they connect with and how they connect with them. As a student or graduate, you want to be more open and flexible, especially if you haven't established a strong network and aren't sure of your career path yet. This will leave you open to as many opportunities as possible. Feel free to stop here and focus on getting this done in the next two weeks—it's that important!

At this point, you should have dozens or hundreds of new connections from across your university. Go through My Network section on your LinkedIn homepage, and look through your connections to admire the network you've built so far.

Next, go through your invitations and the People You May Know section for even more opportunities to extend your network.

You should have a good mix of roles, functions, and experience levels in your network. What do you notice about student profiles compared to the profiles of your professors? Which of these look more complete and more professional? What kinds of words and styles are used by diverse groups of individuals?

For example, how do people in the science departments compare to those in liberal arts? Look at everything in the profiles: their photos, titles, headlines, summaries, experience, and skills. As your network grows, you should be noticing distinctive features in profiles, including quantity and quality of information. One thing you'll likely notice is profiles with media content, such as images, presentations, videos, and links, highlighting the person's work and interests. Best of all, you'll know exactly what you need to add to your profile to outclass your peers and stand out from the competition in your own unique way.

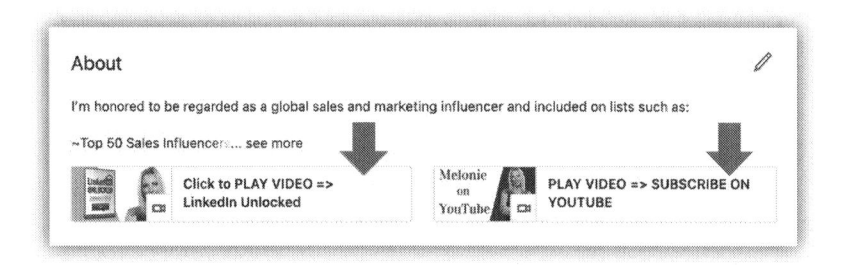

About

I'm honored to be regarded as a global sales and marketing influencer and included on lists such as:

~Top 50 Sales Influencers... see more

Click to PLAY VIDEO => LinkedIn Unlocked

Melonie on YouTube

PLAY VIDEO => SUBSCRIBE ON YOUTUBE

Now that you're one of the most well-connected students on your campus or graduates within your graduating class, it's time to start thinking bigger. Alumni from your university are even more likely than your peers to have active LinkedIn profiles with updated career information.

Go to your university's page on LinkedIn, and visit the alumni section. Look at the most recent graduating classes to see what they studied, what companies they work for, and what work they do.

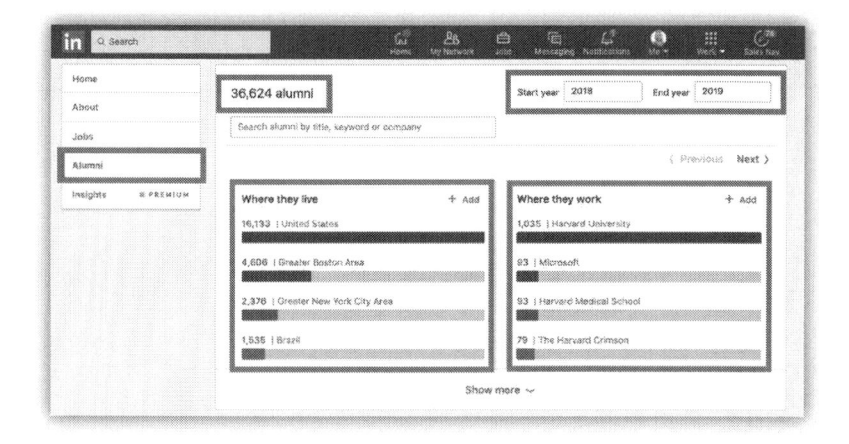

You may notice some trends, such as the top industries and companies hiring graduates from your school—a good indicator of further job opportunities there. Make a list of the top 10 industries, companies, and functions that appear for your university and degree. Do these accurately reflect your career aspirations and expectations? If so, make a list of the top 25 alumni that fit your career criteria.

Spend the next two weeks writing personal connection requests to each of them. Your aim should be to learn something specific from them that can help you understand the local job market and other career opportunities. Eventually, you should be scheduling time to speak with them to continue strengthening the relationships. One of these alumni might hold the particular key that opens the right door for you.

Now that you've spent a month networking within your university and alumni, you should be finding more exciting and relevant content on your LinkedIn homepage. That content is based on the activity of your connections—what they like, comment on, and share. Every single update is an opportunity to engage further with your connections and continue building relationships. By interacting with your connections, you will make yourself known to them. As a result, people will be more likely to pay attention to you when you share something on LinkedIn.

How to Connect with Decision-Makers

Behind every career opportunity is the person(s) making the ultimate decisions about the new hires. In this book, we call them decision-makers. Your task is to (1) identify, (2) understand, and (3) engage with them so they begin regarding you as the strongest candidate.

Many of these recruiters and hiring managers have paid LinkedIn memberships, giving them access to enhanced data and tools. This can be a double-edged sword for students and graduates. If you have a weak presence on LinkedIn, you are less likely to be found. On the other hand, if you approach these paying members intelligently, you'll be much more likely to get a response.

How to find the right information, ask the right questions, and spark conversations

Here are some questions that can guide you through each step of connecting with decision-makers:

1. **Identify**: What are the titles of the decision-makers in the industries and companies you're searching for? Are they responsible for posting jobs on LinkedIn? Whom else do they work with to make hiring decisions, and what do the steps in that process look like?
    Understand: What do these decision-makers care about when looking for new talent? How much influence do they have over the recruitment and hiring process? How do they prefer to be contacted, and how responsive are they when you get in touch?
    Engage: What questions not answered by the job description can you include in your message? What key skills and experience do you have that align with the preferred qualifications of the job? How can you create a positive and lasting impression before and after applying for the job?

When looking for jobs, many people on LinkedIn simply focus on the job post and application, clicking through and submitting forms without ever bothering to get in touch with anyone at that company. This is a very costly mistake for students and graduates.

From the beginning, you may be at a significant disadvantage without even knowing it. This happens not necessarily because you lack some qualifications or experience—many candidates lacking both still get hired—but because you fail to identify, understand, and engage with the people tied to these opportunities. They are only human after all—with fears, flaws, and priorities that could get in your way of getting a job. You need to do everything you can to overcome these obstacles so that you can prepare your approach and, in the end, decide on whether you move forward or move in a new direction.

At times, you will encounter obstacles beyond your control, such as a less-than-adept recruiter. Here are the top ten red flags to watch for in a recruiter, in no particular order:

1. The recruiter doesn't seem to know much about the job they're hiring for and provides vague answers or defers questions to someone else.
2. The recruiter is in a hurry to get answers from you but doesn't care to get to know you beyond those answers.
3. The recruiter is unresponsive online, and when called, they refer you back to the same application pages.
4. The recruiter sounds bored and disinterested, making you wonder about the job and company.
5. The recruiter highlights only the positive aspects of the job and isn't willing to share the challenges.
6. The recruiter promises to get back in touch or come back later with answers to your questions, but you never hear from them again.
7. The recruiter is very chatty but doesn't include much substance about the advertised position or the company.
8. The recruiter makes a mistake but doesn't apologize or even recognize the error.
9. The recruiter is unwilling to introduce you to anyone at the company and gives you excuses about why you can't speak to or meet certain people.

10. The recruiter provides you with incomplete or inaccurate information that affects your interview experience and, ultimately, whether you get the job. If you feel this is happening to you, don't be afraid to speak up and get clarification.

It's crucial you know many things beyond your immediate control can affect your chances of getting the job. Don't be too hard on yourself. The good news is that by using LinkedIn, you can be much better prepared to respond to any eventuality.

You should no longer rely only on what the recruiter says or does. You can now get a closer look at departments, leaders, teams, and individual contributors in the company that can reveal more than any recruiter in that company can. Just don't tell them that!

Once you're ready to engage with decision-makers, follow these suggestions:

Be direct: Explain why you'd like to connect.

Personalize: Include in your message to them what you've learned and admire about them and/or their company.

Be genuine: Go with what you feel and don't overdo it.

Be brief: Keep it short and simple.

Have a call to action: Your goal should be to schedule a quick call with them. Be respectful of their time and tell them you are available at their convenience (in your follow up message, not the initial connection request).

THE ROADMAP TO CONNECTING WITH DECISION MAKERS

When you're ready to engage with decision makers, follow these key suggestions:

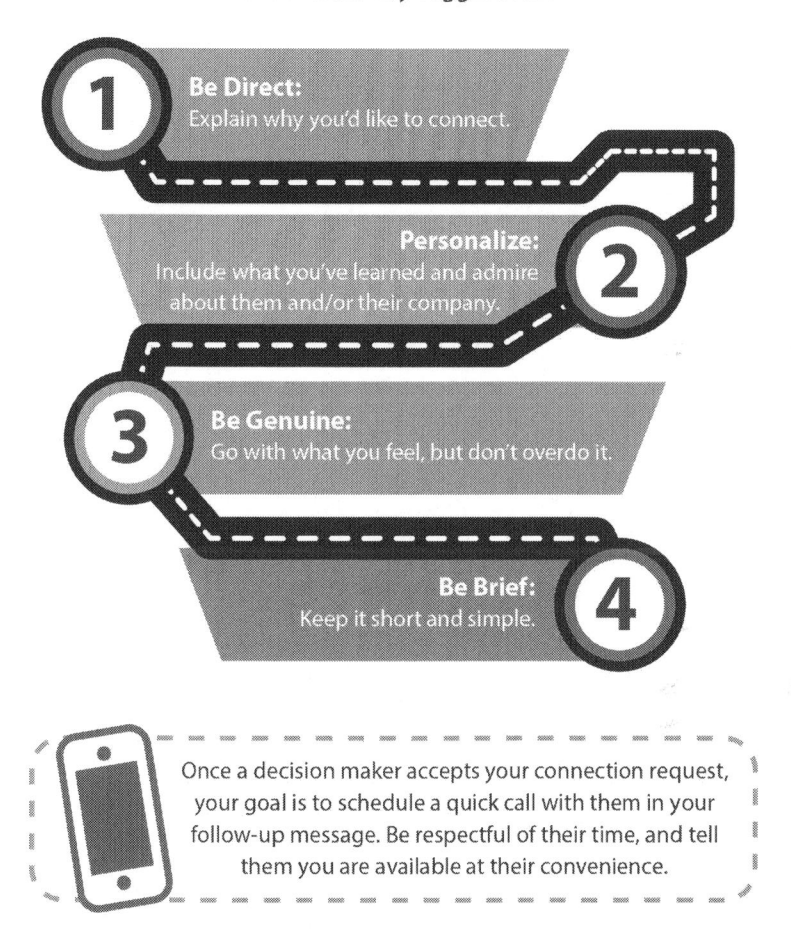

1. Be Direct: Explain why you'd like to connect.

2. Personalize: Include what you've learned and admire about them and/or their company.

3. Be Genuine: Go with what you feel, but don't overdo it.

4. Be Brief: Keep it short and simple.

> Once a decision maker accepts your connection request, your goal is to schedule a quick call with them in your follow-up message. Be respectful of their time, and tell them you are available at their convenience.

Examples of questions to ask:

"Hi Victor, I noticed you've been a sales manager in tech companies for the past eight years. I was wondering what you look for when hiring new team members. Would you have 15 minutes next week to discuss that at a time that's convenient for you?"

"Hi Angela, I see you're recruiting for the graduate program from <insert university>, and I'm very interested as I'm confident this aligns well with my experience and career goals. Are you free to talk about it for ten minutes sometime this week?"

"Hi Jennifer, I really enjoyed the article you shared this morning. I'm also excited about the possibilities to cure cancer in the future. I see you joined <insert company name> as an intern. Would you be open to sharing what you did to get a full-time position there? I'm trying to do something similar, and it would be a great help to me."

In the next chapter, we'll explain more about messaging tactics, but before we move on, let's explore how to start authentic conversations on LinkedIn that can lead you to the right opportunities.

On your LinkedIn homepage, you'll notice a lot of people having many conversations on a range of topics. It's time for you to dig in and get involved.

You can start by going through some of the more popular conversations, where you'll have a good chance of being exposed to both good and bad examples of engagement on LinkedIn. Yes, we'll be the first to admit there are some very poor comments and content that don't do anyone much good. Mostly, however, you'll find some relevant and engaging content and comments that spark new ideas and conversations. This is your place for inspiration!

Go through your homepage right now and look for two-three conversations relevant to your interests and career aspirations. Who posted the update? What are they saying or asking? What link or content did they include? What has been the response from other members so far?

Now, start thinking about what you could add to this conversation. Feel free to like or comment to start building up your activity on LinkedIn. Increasing your activity increases your chances of being noticed by the right person or decision-maker. Do this on a daily basis from now on.

Did you know you can also use #hashtags on LinkedIn? Go ahead and try it. By using a hashtag, you'll enter another area of LinkedIn that highlights specific topics discussed across the world. You can follow these topics to tell LinkedIn what you're interested in, increasing your chances of seeing this content in the future. This is a terrific way to go beyond traditional research and get unparalleled insights into specific topics and trends.

Here are some other ideas on how to spark an authentic conversation:

1. Choose a trending topic or event that relates to your professional interests or area of study. Think about why it's important and what unique insight or angle you can add to the discussion that hasn't been widely considered/covered. Even the most prominent news channels and websites in the world can't do it all. Plus, they have their own agendas that aren't always in the best interest of the public.

2. Think about an assignment or project you're working on that would benefit from the opinions and ideas of your LinkedIn network. Perhaps you'd like to run a survey or ask for feedback on your work. You might be amazed by the responses you receive. We've seen a few students use this to their advantage. Many professionals are very willing to help students or graduates who demonstrate confidence and curiosity. Put yourself and your work out there!

3. Ask your professors and academic staff for ideas on what they consider to be some of the most important topics right now in their fields and subjects. See if they've published or are planning to announce something related to these topics that you can research and contribute towards. This is your chance to see what's already out there. Who on LinkedIn is discussing this, and what are they saying about it? Can you add something new to the conversation? Perhaps there's no one talking about this topic. This is your chance to shine!

4. Go through company pages of the industries you are interested in and see what's being shared here. You'll get a great look at what the company cares about, what challenges it's facing, and what value it's adding. If you've searched far and wide, you'll come across a lot of content that will resonate with you. Pick a few outstanding examples of topics you really care about, and share these with your network. Don't forget to include why you're sharing, and add your own perspective.

5. Go to the profiles of people doing jobs you find exciting, and check their activity and content they are sharing (if any). At this point, it doesn't matter whether they have many views or followers. Focus on what matters to you about the content they're sharing. It can be especially refreshing for that person to see that you've taken the time to read their content and comment on it. If you're not connected, this is a fantastic opportunity to let them know how much you enjoyed what they're sharing in a personalized connection request. You should also follow them to receive notifications every time they share new content so you can continue building a strong relationship.

HOW TO SPARK CONVERSATIONS WITH DECISION MAKERS

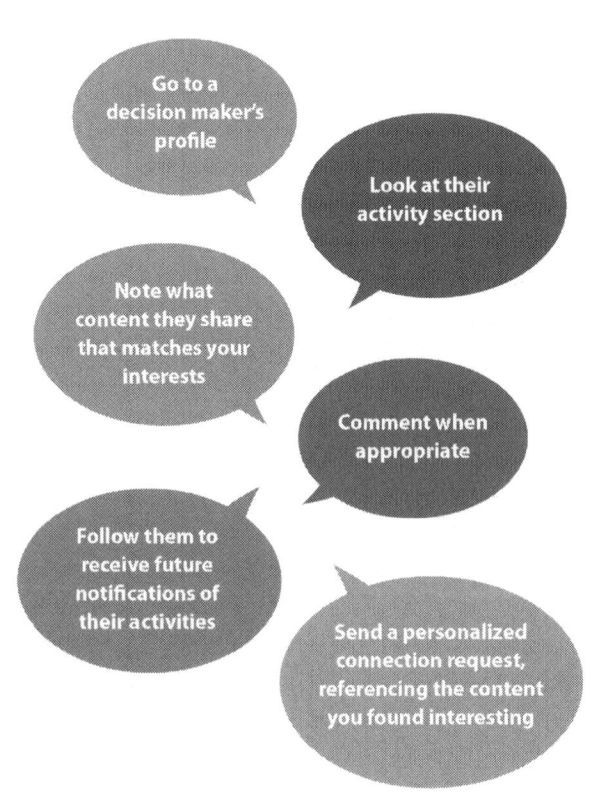

- Go to a decision maker's profile
- Look at their activity section
- Note what content they share that matches your interests
- Comment when appropriate
- Follow them to receive future notifications of their activities
- Send a personalized connection request, referencing the content you found interesting

If you've done everything discussed in this chapter, you should have a much better idea of what it takes to build meaningful relationships on LinkedIn. We hope you have already received some great responses and set up some calls and meetings that could open doors in the very near future.

Please don't miss out on these connections and relationship-building opportunities! We know it won't feel natural reaching out to people you don't know and asking for their time and attention. The good news is most professionals expect to be approached by other professionals on LinkedIn. All you need to do is apply the knowledge we shared with you in this chapter to make your message and approach stand out from the rest. This will be an essential skill for you to learn and get comfortable with throughout your professional life.

Things to focus on in the next seven days:

1. How well connected are you to other students, staff, and faculty at your university on LinkedIn?
2. Have you connected to alumni from your university who are doing the type of work and jobs you're interested in?
3. Are you up to date with the most important people, topics, and trends relevant to the types of jobs you plan to apply for?

Things to do in the next seven days:

1. Connect with 50-100 people from your university and surrounding community.
2. Connect with 25-30 alumni working in the companies and doing the jobs that interest you.
3. Follow at least 10 different topics on LinkedIn using hashtags, and search for relevant people and groups aligned with your interests within the conversation stream.

CHAPTER 8

EFFECTIVE MESSAGING TACTICS TO CONNECT WITH DECISION-MAKERS

In the previous chapter, we talked about recruiters and hiring managers as examples of the decision-makers you need to get to know. For every industry, company, department, function, and role, you need to think bigger. Always ask yourself who the people who can influence and ultimately make the hiring decision are. Without knowing this, you are just like everyone else who is merely hoping someone will like their application enough to offer them an interview.

As a student and graduate, you are less likely to be noticed than many other highly qualified candidates with many years of experience. You need to go above and beyond to connect with the right people and understand what they care about because it's unlikely to be obvious.

To do this, you first need to understand how connection requests work on LinkedIn. Technically speaking, it's quite simple. Many profiles will have a Connect button under the person's photo and headline. Before you connect with someone, you need to be interested in building a professional relationship with that person, and you need to take the time to understand what would be of value to them.

You need to be extra mindful about the way you approach these influencers and decision-makers. You don't want for your connection request to be lost in a flood of generic connection requests they receive from others daily. Make sure you personalize your connection requests, giving the person you are contacting a reason to reply to you.

Also, reaching out to them looking for a job isn't the best or most tactful way to get a conversation started. These very busy professionals are experienced in spotting laziness and a lack of authenticity and prefer to hear from someone who has taken the time to truly understand their needs and the needs of their businesses. If you want your connection request to be accepted, think about it from their perspective, not your own.

How to Send a Connection Request That Gets Accepted

How NOT to use the all-powerful Connect button:

1. Don't do it for the sake of numbers. It's better for you to have 200 amazing connections than 1000 random ones you don't really care or know much about.

2. Don't click Connect hoping to get noticed if you don't plan to send a personalized request, telling them why you'd like to connect.

3. Don't include too much in your connection request as you may come off as if you're trying too hard and end up sounding desperate. You can follow up with another message later. Plus, you have only 300 characters to write your connection request message, so you must use them wisely.

4. Don't expect a written response to your connection requests even when they get accepted, and don't be too hard on yourself if you never hear back from the person you wrote to. They may be getting too many requests every day and are either ignoring them or too busy to bother writing back.

5. Don't immediately ask for something once your connection request is accepted. Send a short thank-you message, and let your new connection know you value the opportunity to learn something specific from them and the content they share on LinkedIn.

Effective Messaging Tactics to Connect with Decision-Makers

HOW TO SEND A PERSONALIZED LINKEDIN CONNECTION REQUEST

STEP 1

Name · 2nd
Senior Vice President
Amsterdam Area, Netherlands · 500+ connections · Contact info

Connect | View in Sales Navigator | More...

CRH
Université libre de Bruxelles

STEP 2

You can customize this invitation ✕

LinkedIn members are more likely to accept invitations that include a personal note.

Add a note | Send now

STEP 3

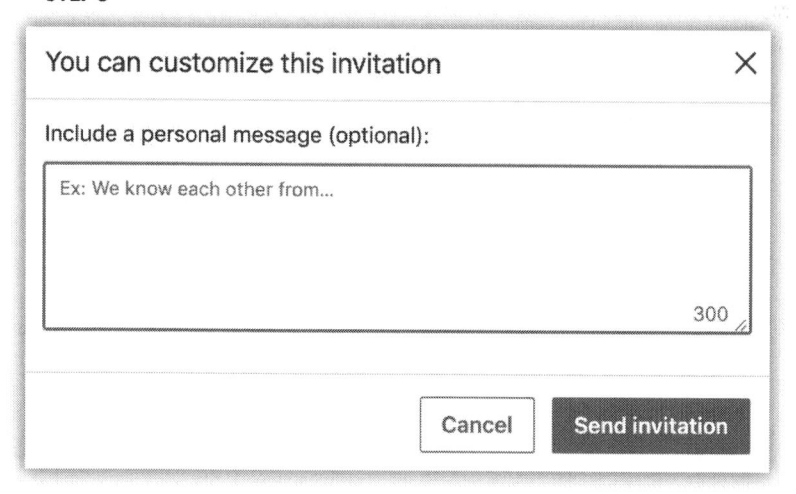

You can customize this invitation ✕

Include a personal message (optional):

Ex: We know each other from...

300

Cancel | Send invitation

91

If you don't feel confident yet or have much luck with your connection requests, here is a good alternative. Follow the people you care about as they can't stop you from following them. By clicking the Follow button, you'll show them you're interested in what they share without expecting to build formal professional relationships with them—at least not yet. This means you'll see their posts in your LinkedIn newsfeed and learn what they care about and how they help others in their networks.

You could start engaging with them by liking and sharing their posts or articles, commenting on the ones that resonate with you, and using one of the topics they've written about to find a unique way to get into a conversation with them. What perspective do you bring that they're missing or haven't considered? How are other people reacting to their posts? Does someone have the attention of the author allowing you to jump into the discussion respectfully? Has the author asked a question you can answer? Could you reframe the question to help them ask an even better question?

Every great professional is open to constructive feedback, and they love when others in their network build upon what they're sharing. Be that person! You may just end up connecting with a significant expert and influencer. After all, they had to start somewhere too. They probably did many of the things we've just shared with you here, even if they weren't feeling confident. It's better to speak up and refine your methods than to remain silent and never learn how to get better.

What to Say and Do After You Connect

You may be thinking, *How is this actually going to help me get a job? Just because I connect with decision-makers and professionals on LinkedIn and follow what they're doing doesn't mean I'll find the job of my dreams, right?*

If that's all you do with the connection, you are probably correct. However, it's definitely a step in the right direction. You'll come to realize that connecting on LinkedIn is the easy part once you see the real value of those connections for years to come.

Here is what to say and do in the first few months after you connect:

1. Send your new connection a quick thank-you message. In it, tell them why you value having them in your network, what you've learned from them, and what you hope to learn from them in the future that will help you achieve your goals. Be concise and precise. You want to be memorable without asking for too much at the start.

2. Look through their profile and check their latest updates. What are they liking, commenting on, and sharing? Reviewing their activity section will often reveal some of their personality, interests, values, and activities. Take note of anything you identify with and can use to build rapport, ask them questions, and get their attention. It's okay to wait a few days or weeks before you message them again, but don't let too much time pass. Remind them who you are when you message them. For example:

"Hi Sarah, we connected a few weeks ago when I read your article on how to solve the productivity crisis hurting the UK economy. It's something I'm very passionate about and noticed that you attended an event yesterday where you were a speaker. I'd love to know of any other conferences happening this year you could recommend that are tackling this topic. I'd love to get more exposure to other professionals who care about the same things. Thank you for your time."

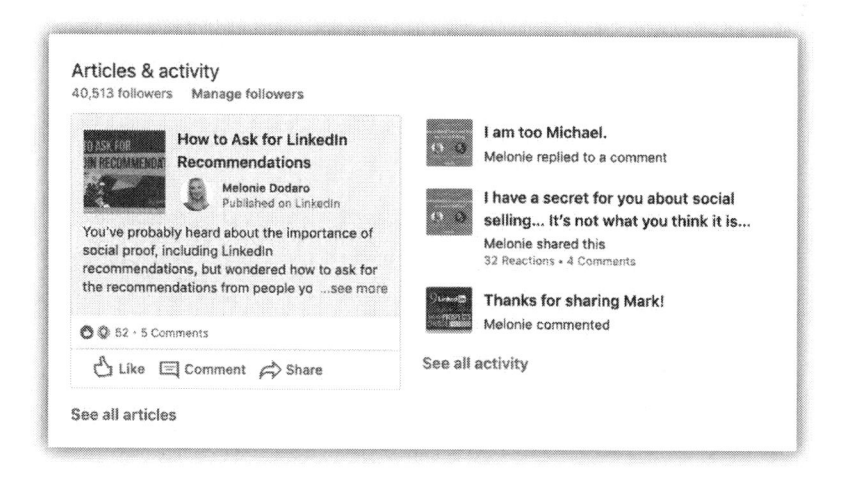

![Articles & activity section screenshot showing 40,513 followers, with posts including "How to Ask for LinkedIn Recommendations" by Melonie Dodaro, "I am too Michael.", "I have a secret for you about social selling... It's not what you think it is...", and "Thanks for sharing Mark!"]

3. Go to the Endorsements and Recommendations sections of their profile to see what they're really good at as well as what others have recognized about them and their work. Which of their skills has the most endorsements? Is this a skill you have? Make sure it's on your list, and ask people you've studied or worked with to endorse you. Which of their recommendations stand out from the rest? Use what you read there to ask them about their experience. It'll help you understand what they did to achieve a certain benchmark and gain recognition from their bosses, colleagues, and customers.

4. Find out whom else they're connected with—especially in the same company or industry—using it as an opportunity to discover and build relationships with the right people more efficiently. Could they introduce you to someone on their team or to that senior project manager working in the same office? Maybe you notice they're well connected to digital marketing people in your city, and you'd love to understand what entry-level positions you should consider as a graduate. Feel free to name-drop when appropriate. For example:

    "Hi, Jonathan! We connected a few months ago, and you answered my questions about the graduate recruitment process. I learned a lot from you. Thanks again! I'm now considering marketing roles at <insert company name> and noticed you're connected to <insert name> who is a Senior Marketing Manager there. Do you know him well? If so, could you introduce me to him here on LinkedIn? I'd appreciate 10-15 minutes of his time as I saw he's hiring an assistant and I believe I fit the qualifications. If this isn't possible, I still appreciate your time and hope we can speak again soon. Thank you!"

5. Share a relevant post or article with them you believe they would find interesting. This will be more meaningful if it's something you personally found or wrote with them in mind. Be genuine with your approach, and don't choose anything that is poorly written, too controversial, or lengthy. Let them know why you believe it's important and valuable.

Effective Outreach Strategies

Getting the attention of busy professionals is not easy, especially when they don't know you and don't think you could offer them anything of value. It can seem like an ineffective process when you put in the effort to reach out but get only a few helpful responses. DO NOT GIVE UP!

We've been saying it throughout this book, but it's worth repeating again: you cannot afford to take this stuff personally and beat yourself up about it. As a student, you were probably never taught this. Perhaps no one has ever encouraged you to do it before, so give yourself three to six months to build your LinkedIn network more strategically, even if all you have is 5-10 minutes a day. Keep clicking those Connect and Follow buttons; keep writing those personalized connection request messages; and keep clicking that Send button until it becomes completely comfortable and even exciting.

With hundreds of millions of LinkedIn members, you can never say you've tried everyone and everything. Take comfort in the knowledge that there is always more you can be doing to get noticed by the right decision-makers.

Don't forget all the people surrounding those recruiters and hiring managers. Even if you have trouble getting a response from someone in the marketing department, that doesn't mean you should ignore someone from the sales or support team in the same company—they could introduce you to the right person. Just be authentic and professional with your approach so they know what you're after from the very beginning.

How to Write Like a Business Professional

Writing those short connection requests on LinkedIn is a great way to practice a different style of writing from the one you used in your academic work. Many students and graduates feel they need to be overly formal, long-winded, and even apologetic when writing to professionals. This is unfortunate since extreme formality can be perceived as desperation. You may come across as trying too hard to please or as compensating for your lack of skills or experience.

Trying to include too much about yourself or what you want is a quick way to be ignored as well. Imagine that the recipient of your message is reading it on their smartphone with many other distractions vying for their time. They shouldn't have to scroll several times to go through long, chunky paragraphs. Ideally, they wouldn't have to scroll at all.

Lastly, please don't apologize for taking up their time, and don't be too submissive with your style of writing. You'll appear weak and may not be taken seriously. Many professionals like to see students and graduates showing initiative and confidence even if they lack other credentials.

Here's what to focus on when writing like a business professional:

1. Write clearly and precisely with as few words as possible so it's easy to read.
2. Be polite and positive, but don't sound overly formal or intellectual.
3. Make sure to elaborate with real examples rather than ideas and theories.
4. Use an active voice rather than a passive one.
5. Use well-constructed opinions, but don't bombard with facts.

What to focus on in the next seven days:

1. What will make it more likely for decision-makers to accept your connection requests?
2. What are the best ways to follow up after a decision-maker accepts your connection request?
3. How can you identify other influencers within the same company, department, location, and team to whom you could be introduced?

What to do in the next seven days:

1. Spot 2-3 opportunities to engage with each decision-maker through specific topics of conversations related to the content they're sharing or other activity on their profile.

2. Send a follow-up message to each decision-maker who has accepted your connection request to start a conversation that leads to a call, meeting, and eventually interview!

3. Always ask each decision-maker for introductions to other people and/or people they recommend you should speak to who can influence the hiring process.

CHAPTER 9

ENGAGE WITH YOUR NETWORK TO STAND OUT FROM THE CROWD

Once you connect and build strong relationships with decision-makers and influencers, it's important to keep those relationships not only alive but thriving. LinkedIn will remind you on a regular basis when it's someone's birthday, work anniversary, or the anniversary of your connection. Use this information as an opportunity to get in touch with your connections.

On the other hand, don't rely on it too much. Most of what you send to your connections should be more meaningful than a simple *Congrats!* If you've followed our advice so far, you should have the right number of valuable relationships with plenty of opportunities to stay in touch with them.

Staying top of mind and building credibility with your connections will help you:

1. be in the right place at the right time with the right people
2. become a memorable name and face, attracting the proper attention
3. remind others what you stand for and what you're looking for
4. understand what really matters and how best to approach others
5. attract recruiters and hiring managers looking for someone like you.

By now, you should understand why having a great profile, searching and applying for jobs, and connecting with people isn't enough to forge your path to success. Almost anyone can accomplish that. What is more unusual is a candidate who stands out because of his or her actions and the content they share with their network.

It's easy to add a bunch of skills, nice numbers, and fancy achievements to your profile. What is unique is someone who is living and breathing their passion, made evident through the content they share, the articles they write, and the recommendations they receive from others. Nothing screams authenticity like hearing others promoting and celebrating your values and actions.

Don't underestimate the value of a recommendation your professor can give you. The same goes for a recommendation from your manager at your internship site. You can even thank them and share what you learned from them by @mentioning them on LinkedIn. That will set you apart from the crowd.

Focus on not only what you can get from the connections you've built on LinkedIn but also what value you can offer them. If you want to come across as someone who genuinely cares about helping other people, start with giving rather than asking.

Your goal will be to discover what resonates with your network and find ways to engage with its members. This can be as simple as offering a few words of encouragement in the form of a quote that has helped you during difficult times. Or you might share a carefully crafted article that helps companies understand what your generation thinks about their products and services. Look at what your connections are sharing and talking about, and make sure you choose relevant topics to post on. Don't forget to personalize your updates and add your own perspective.

Another excellent way to engage with your network is to ask questions that will lead to answers relevant to a large group of people. For example, you can ask your network what their favorite qualities of great leaders are or the most useful career advice they ever received.

You can start by @mentioning some of your peers and other people you know well. They will receive a notification as if you sent them a direct message, increasing your chances of getting a response. Perhaps you have a favorite colleague, professor, or staff member that could help you get started with this type of engagement. By tagging the right people, you ensure that your post is seen not only by them but also by their networks, dramatically expanding your reach. Asking the right questions will set you up for success, no matter what job you do.

5 QUESTIONS TO CREATE ENGAGEMENT

1 What is the most important quality of a leader?

2 What is the most helpful career advice you have ever received?

3 What is one tip you would give to a recent grad looking for a job?

4 What is the best piece of advice you wished you knew before graduating that you could give to a young person today?

5 What is the #1 issue that needs to be addressed in the [insert industry]?

Many students who have grown up using social media still struggle to apply their social media skills in the professional sphere, LinkedIn in particular. You might be one of them. You might feel as if you need to be overly cautious about what you share. Or if you are still not sure what you want to do after university, you may feel the need to wait to build a large professional network, connecting and engaging only with a few people in the meantime.

If you're serious about getting the full value of LinkedIn, you cannot wait until you feel 100% confident. It's likely that as you start posting content and engaging in conversations, the first few weeks or months on LinkedIn will result in mixed success and emotions. You might think that because your post received only limited views and resulted in zero comments, it was a complete waste of time, but that's not what matters at the beginning of your journey.

We had written dozens of articles and spent many months sharing them before they ever reached thousands of views. It isn't a popularity or numbers game. What is important is that (a) you share content that genuinely matters to you and (b) you pay attention to the engagement you get on your posts so that you can keep getting better at it.

How to Stay Top of Mind and Build Credibility

We suggest you choose five to ten of your connections per week, preferably the ones who are more active on LinkedIn, and decide how you'll get in touch with them. If you haven't connected with them for awhile, look through their profiles and activity sections to see what they've been doing lately. Does anything jump out at you or sound interesting? Have they started a new job? Are they sharing exciting updates about their work? Do you see a pattern with the type of topics and content they share?

Once you've chosen your five to ten connections, here's how to stay top of mind and build credibility:

1. Send your connection a message, asking them how they're doing and letting them know why you are getting in touch. For example:

    "Hi Andrew, it's great to see all your travel updates. I especially enjoyed seeing the work you've been doing lately in Asia with your new office. I was just getting back in touch to see if you had any plans to visit <insert your city> again. I'd be happy to invite you for a coffee to chat about my studies and plans after I graduate that align closely with the developments you shared about your expansion in the Chinese market. In any case, I hope to stay in touch and keep learning about your work. Thank you!"

2. Choose something they shared recently, and add a comment. For example:

"I agree that artificial intelligence and machine learning are going to disrupt the traditional ways of working, but at the same time, I've seen research that points to a greater need for human skills and experience to work alongside this technology. It will be important that people are able to work with these machines and that they can step in when the machines aren't able to make sense of what the right human response should be. I look forward to reading more about your work!"

3. Find an article that relates to the work they do, and share it with them or tag them in a post. For example:

"I read this great story about the way innovative retail shops are creating in-store experiences that customers love by mixing traditional practices with fun technology. I thought you might enjoy reading it as Director of Customer Experience and may want to add to the conversation, talking about what your company is also doing to stay ahead of the game. Look forward to hearing from you!"

Curate Content That Your Network Will Value

Sharing unique content and advice is a powerful way to become influential within your network. This is especially true if you're the creator and not just the curator of that content. Original content is a lot harder to come by these days as almost everything shared or published has been heavily repurposed. This isn't necessarily bad, but it does mean that your original content may be held to higher scrutiny than any other content you post on LinkedIn. We'll talk a lot more about this in the next chapter.

While creating your own content can make a significant impact on your overall career development, you don't need to do it just yet if you're still finding your way around LinkedIn. We suggest first you become comfortable and confident curating high-quality content from a variety of different sources and experiences you encounter throughout your day.

Inspiration to Get You Started

Here are some ideas to get you started:

1. Research recently published books, and share a relevant insight from one of them.

2. Read the daily newspapers, and share your views on a trending topic.

3. Ask your professor whether they're comfortable being quoted, and if they say yes, share the quote with your network.

4. Scroll through Twitter to find interesting and relevant discussions.

5. Read your favorite magazine, and add your opinion about a specific story.

6. Share images and videos covering projects and events that bring your work to life.

The more content you curate and share, the more you'll realize that every single day is filled with experiences that matter to thousands of others. You don't have to wait to be hit with a lightning bolt of inspiration to share on LinkedIn. Most of the things we share naturally arise from our curiosity and moments of quiet contemplation during a long walk or commute. Posting should take you only a few minutes, so don't overthink it. Keep your target audience in mind, and if you know others will enjoy and find your updates valuable, share them.

As a student or graduate preparing for and settling into your life after university, you want to make sure that most of the content you share has a purpose behind it—getting you that dream job or furthering your career!

We're not suggesting you over-analyze every single update you post, but you *should* keep in mind that when you engage with your network, you're ultimately creating perceptions, and your reputation will be working for you or against you whether you know it or not.

Always ask yourself how a recruiter or hiring manager would perceive what you're sharing. Of course, it's impossible to know all their biases, interests, dislikes, and personalities, but your posts can tell them a lot about your professionalism and your values. You want to be perceived as someone who is interesting, confident, and knowledgeable with strong written communication skills, which can be easily conveyed through your LinkedIn updates.

Business mogul Warren Buffet has some surprising advice on how to increase one's net worth by 50%. He recommends you hone your communication skills, both written and verbal. He said, "If you can't communicate… nothing happens."[14]

How do you know you're on the right track? You know it when you start attracting the right people who can offer you the right opportunities. It's a satisfying feeling seeing others commenting on what you shared.

Make sure to show respect and appreciation for people who have taken the time to engage with your content. Your responses will make you stand out more than anything else you do on LinkedIn. Even a quick thank-you note or a short reply letting them know you're listening is enough. But if they've sparked a new idea or perspective, don't hesitate to start a healthy debate or discussion. This can be an excellent opportunity for others in your network to engage with you by adding their perspectives. In the process, you might be forging new paths to your next career opportunity without even realizing it.

---

14 Andy Serwer, "Warren Buffett Shares His Keys to Success," *Yahoo Finance* video, 2:32, April 18, 2019, *https://news.yahoo.com/warren-buffett-shares-keys-success-134329028.html*

Things to focus on in the next seven days:

1. Which of your connections should you get in touch with?
2. What have you recently seen or read that you think would be valuable to share on LinkedIn?
3. Whom can you @mention, and what kinds of questions can you ask to get comments on your posts?

Things to do in the next seven days:

1. Choose 5-10 connections per week to get in touch with and send them short messages on LinkedIn. Don't underestimate the value of checking in and keeping in touch!
2. Choose a topic you love that's trending in the news and widely discussed, and tell your LinkedIn network why it matters to you.
3. Choose two or more people you know well, and let them know you would like to @mention them on LinkedIn to start a healthy and productive conversation on a relevant topic.

CHAPTER 10

MOVING FROM CONTENT CURATOR TO CONTENT CREATOR

We hope by now you've spent a few weeks finding and sharing useful and interesting content on LinkedIn. If you haven't, we encourage you to spend at least two to three weeks doing this before writing your first article. After following our recommendations from previous chapters, you should be seeing a good amount of engagement that already has led to some opportunities for you to build better and stronger relationships on LinkedIn.

As you curate valuable content, you also learn what it takes to write and create content of your own. Look back through your activity to see which topics you've mentioned more than others. Are these the ones you know and enjoy the most? Continue expanding on these topics! Begin focusing on becoming more specialized and delving deeper into the content that interests you the most. It's likely that what you enjoy and consider important also resonates with many other people.

In this chapter, we explore the transition from gathering and sharing the content of others to writing and sharing your own content. It's a big step for most people on LinkedIn, and only a tiny percentage write their own articles. We hope by now you see that content creation is a tremendous opportunity for your professional development and career advancement.

Finding Your Voice on LinkedIn

Most of the influential leaders on LinkedIn share their thoughts and feelings with the world. Bill Gates, Satya Nadella, Richard Branson, Jeff Weiner, Oprah Winfrey, and Arianna Huffington are a few examples of people you should take some time to read. You'll start getting a sense of the different writing styles and topics relevant to millions of people. You may think that because they're rich, famous, and lead thousands of people, it's easy for them to pump out dozens of articles and books regularly. The truth is, they've been working hard and smart well before any of them were millionaires/billionaires, well-known outside of their companies, and managing other people.

Everyone starts somewhere. Writing your first article on LinkedIn could be the first step toward fulfilling your own marvelous destiny or, at the very least, getting noticed by recruiters and hiring managers!

Take a moment to write down ten things you notice about the articles you've read so far. What is it about the headline that grabs your attention?

What's in the first paragraph, middle, and end of the article? How long is it, and how long did it take you to read it? How is it formatted to make it more reader-friendly? Does the author include any data and graphs to back up their main points? Do they tell a compelling story that elicits some kind of emotion?

Once you note your observations, write next to each point how you'll use it to help you with your own article. These tips and reminders will be your cheat sheet from now on. Keep it next to you every time you start writing your next article.

Catchy headline: Create some intrigue that makes the reader want to click to read more. For example, "Surprising Responses I Got From Recruiters When I Asked About Workplace Culture" or "How I Got My First Job Without Applying or Interviewing."

Beautiful image: Choose something original and meaningful rather than the typical stock photography available online. Make sure the image is clear and reflects what you're writing about, perhaps revealing a scene from your story.

Short paragraphs: Don't have long sentences and chunky blocks of text that make reading your article feel like a chore, especially when people are on their phones. Make sure to divide the article using subtitles, images, or quotes when shifting to another idea, topic, or question. People often scan articles before they decide to read them, so make sure to lay out your articles in a reader-friendly manner.

Links: Include links to your other articles at the end to encourage readers to engage further if they enjoyed your writing.

Short bio: At the end of the article, tell the reader who you are and what you're passionate about to help the reader understand why you are writing about this topic. Encourage readers to get in touch with you if they would like to discuss these topics or need advice about a related subject.

HOW TO CREATE COMPELLING CONTENT

1 Create a compelling headline/title for your content.

2 Add sub headers to your post to let readers know what they'll learn in each section.

3 Keep paragraphs short at 2-3 lines (or 75 to 100 words) to make your content more readable.

4 Include visual elements in your post, such as images, graphics and videos, to make your content more engaging.

5 Use bullet points and lists to break up your text, making your post easy to read.

6 Link to other valuable resources within your post to provide readers with additional information without making your post too long or difficult to consume.

7 Include a short and appropriate call to action at the bottom of your post to tell readers what you want them to do next.

8 Have one or more people read through the blog post to help eliminate errors.

Look at the top three topics you want to focus on. They should be closely related to the content you've been curating and sharing on LinkedIn. This will make it a lot easier for you to decide what you'll write about and how you'll write it.

The most important thing to remember is if you've picked topics you're genuinely passionate about, you should be enjoying the overall process and results. Of course, this doesn't mean you'll be in a state of wonderful flow 100% of the time, where all the right ideas and words go straight from your head to the page in front of you. But if you are interested in your subject matter, it should be easier for you to get over any writer's block that will inevitably come up in the writing process. Stepping away from writing for a bit also helps. Fresh eyes often bring new ideas and perspectives.

You should also focus on what you already know so you don't feel as if you have to do vast amounts of research to write an article. Your first article on LinkedIn should lie at the intersection of what you know, what you're good at, and what the world needs.

At this point, it's not about being an expert on your topic but rather knowing enough to share an educated opinion with a few interesting personal insights. Perhaps you have a story of how social media can influence gang violence, and you'd like to offer alternative ways to tackle the problems of disenfranchised youth. Or you want to bring attention to mental health issues affecting students so you can encourage university staff and healthcare providers to be more considerate. If you feel strongly about topics affecting the lives of thousands or millions of people, you're already well on your way to becoming an influential content creator.

Repurposing Your Projects, Essays, and Other University Work

We bet as a student you've done a good amount of writing, whether it's book reports, science projects, or essays. The good news is you can use your past work and your aspirations as sources of ideas for LinkedIn articles.

It might seem strange at first to post your student work on LinkedIn after reading what other professionals share, but our goal with this book is to change that. We believe the happiest employees are the ones who take pride in the work they do, and that's why we want to encourage you to start thinking and doing the same while you are a student.

You won't be super passionate or even remotely interested in everything you've done as a student, and that's okay. You'll find that even the best jobs have less than exciting or interesting aspects. What you need to do is ask yourself what kinds of subjects you found most fulfilling and where you felt most alive. These are the topics that sparked your curiosity and encouraged you to ask questions and think differently.

Now, what kind of work have you done or are doing on these topics? What is relevant and trending today that's connected to your studies? Delve deeper than your textbooks; go farther than your lectures; and explore wider than a simple Google search. By using LinkedIn, you can see the people and organizations representing exactly what you're learning, with the added benefit of it being current and updated in real time.

Find other sources of opinion that haven't been represented in your classroom or textbooks. Find industry leaders and role models who are stretching the conventional ways of thinking, working, and living. Read other articles that redefine standards and expectations so that you can become more comfortable doing the same when it's time to start challenging what others have taught you.

How Publishing Articles on LinkedIn Can Help You Attract the Right Audience

It might be obvious at this point, but one of the great benefits of publishing on LinkedIn is its ability to help you attract the right audience. LinkedIn's power to promote your professional brand is almost unmatched by any other online publishing platform. Where else do you find this great number of professionals from across many different countries, companies, and industries gathered in one place to see your content?

While Facebook and Instagram come to mind, and they certainly help many businesses, they are not used in ways that can help you get discovered by a future employer. If you're in the artistic and creative space, perhaps you'll beg to differ, and we would agree with you. However, we would suggest using a combination of different social media channels, including LinkedIn, to expand on those fantastic photos you took on Instagram.

I recently chose one photographer over another because of the way he described his projects in articles as well as the recommendations his clients left on his LinkedIn profile—even though his prices were 40% higher! You might know how to take lovely photos and post them on Instagram, but it's even better if you have a great story and people to back you up.

The level of effort to write good quality articles is high, but so are the rewards. As you look through other profiles, you'll see how prominent articles appear and how easy they are to spot. Although the number of people publishing on LinkedIn has increased in the last several years, it's still very low. These articles make a clear visual difference and attract attention unlike anything else on a person's profile.

When publishing on LinkedIn, do not worry about getting large numbers of readers and followers. This is especially true if you've just started writing and publishing. The point of this exercise is not to attract a large audience; it's to attract the RIGHT audience. By that, we mean the kind of people whom you want to work with and the ones ultimately responsible for helping you get a job.

Just think about what a difference it would make when, after reviewing your resume, a manager decides to search for you on LinkedIn. They can see you not only have a stellar profile but also published articles relevant to the job and the type of problems they work on solving. Say they decide to read one of your articles and are impressed by your level of knowledge and sophistication. No other job candidate they've reviewed has made such a great impression, and they haven't even met you yet!

This is precisely what you want to focus on when writing your first article. If you could get only one person to read your article from start to finish, who would it be? I bet if you're searching for jobs, that person would be the one responsible for hiring you. They are the ones you're writing for. By focusing on one person instead of trying to please hundreds or thousands, you simplify the task of writing for the right audience. Your writing will come across as clear and purposeful as you know exactly whom it's for and what it's meant to achieve. Now you need to make sure the right people see it!

Since you've written this article with a particular person in mind, don't be shy about sharing it with them. You don't need to tell them the article was written mainly for them. Just tell them why you'd love for them to read it. Does it align with the work they're doing? Does it share a perspective they might find interesting or helpful? Are you seeking their validation and feedback on a new development in the industry?

You want to make sure it's clear that you want them to read it and that it's positioned to be for their benefit. If they tell you they found it interesting, why not ask them to share your article with their network?

Are you starting to see the bigger picture? Writing for and sharing an article with one person can give you a chance to get that article in front of other people, similar to that first person. All it takes is connecting to the right person to attract the right audience. You'll soon come to appreciate this chain reaction on LinkedIn. It is heavily dependent on building strong relationships with the right people so that they can promote the brand of YOU.

Showcase What You Know and Care About

As you start publishing your articles on LinkedIn, you might find you're interested in certain topics more than others. Maybe when you first started, you thought you were really enthusiastic about innovations in cancer research, but later you realized you're more interested in nutrition science as it can help people live healthier lives and avoid or mitigate cancer in the first place. Perhaps you chose to dive into a complex and rapidly changing subject, such as artificial intelligence or blockchain, and don't yet feel confident writing about it. Sure, you love reading about the topic, but have you really worked on it or experienced it enough to write about it?

You should start with what you already know and care about when publishing on LinkedIn. How do you determine whether you know enough about a subject? Here is your yardstick: You should know and care about this topic so much that you would barely need to do any additional research to complete an article on it.

It might feel strange and uncomfortable for many of you, especially if you're a student, but it's the best way to get you to write something that represents who you are and not who you think you need to be. Don't get us wrong, that doesn't mean you shouldn't research before writing. You can still do that. But remember, everyone has a story to tell. You just need to find yours and write about it without worrying about the number of likes and followers and without depending on the words and thoughts of others.

Just write on that blank page as though you were having a conversation with your best friend or loved one. You've had those, right? Well, writing is just another style of conveying those same thoughts and emotions. Let loose, but still ask someone to proofread your work! It's good to come back to it one more time. The best articles we published were not rushed. By letting yourself to mull over an article before coming back to it one last time, you can turn a good piece of content into a great one.

One of the great byproducts of writing is it can be a wonderful exercise of self-discovery, leading you through many twists and turns and sparking your imagination. It could be that through the simple effort of writing on LinkedIn, you start uncovering what you really know. More importantly, you start discovering what you would like to know more about. The more you write, the more you'll surprise and delight yourself by your articles. And the more you feel excited by your writing, the more you'll care about what you write, helping you write even better. All of this started because you decided to begin with what was already on your mind and pursue what was in your heart.

Produce Original Work to Establish Authority and Credibility

Even if you don't do any formal research, your writing will still be influenced by what you've learned from others. It's not necessarily a bad thing. What is important is you find a way to write in your own voice and with your own perspectives, supporting your points by facts rather than just opinions. There is nothing wrong with expressing your opinions, but you'll gain more authority and credibility by backing up what you write with nearly indisputable proof.

How do you produce original work?

Earlier, we talked about writing what you know and care about. That's how to get started and get noticed. By producing your own content, you demonstrate you have the skills and creativity to write on LinkedIn. You might find that some people relate to your personal stories and see you as a source of inspiration.

Take Miguel's journey as a LinkedIn writer as an example:

"When I first started writing on LinkedIn, I was proud to have even a few friends, colleagues, and family members leaving lovely comments on my articles. This boosted my confidence and got me excited to write my next article, even if only a few people commented on it. And remember, the vast majority of people do not comment, but that doesn't mean they haven't read it.

After doing this for many months, I started getting a little more serious about my writing. It was nice that some of my first articles were grabbing the attention of some of the people I knew well, but I also wanted to write about other things. So, I focused on covering topics that were related to my work and shared what I had learned from these different work experiences. Eventually, my articles were read by more and more people. I was starting to get featured on LinkedIn under different categories—unfortunately, they have since changed this feature, making it harder to get featured—and saw some of my articles getting thousands of views in a relatively short amount of time. I had never seen so many people reading my writing! The increasing number of views inspired me to continue publishing my articles.

I was producing original work on topics I knew no one had written about before—at least not in the way I was writing it. Do you want to know how I knew? I knew it because before choosing a headline for my articles or deciding my main points, I searched to see what was already out there on the topic. I wasn't necessarily researching what to write. Instead, I was looking for what had already been written to ensure I was keeping my points as original as possible. I wanted to make sure my work didn't come across as a rehash of another article or a summary of ideas already widely shared.

Soon enough, people I didn't know were reaching out to me after reading my articles and sharing their thoughts. It was an overwhelmingly positive and enriching experience.

Of course, your writing won't please everyone, and sometimes it will even disappoint some people, driving them to leave a negative comment.

Don't worry! As long as you're writing with conviction and are grounded in what you know and care about, you shouldn't fear what others think—embrace them instead.

Some of my best responses have been to my detractors—the people who openly disagreed with me—where I provided further clarification or reiterated what I had written. You'll be surprised by the number of people who might read the headline of your article and skim through the rest, missing all the important points. Yet, others who disagree may provide handy insights and other ways of thinking that may be very persuasive. You might even be proven wrong. Gasp! This is your time to shine and show your professional side. Take all of this as a learning experience, and let your guard down. Accept that at some point you might discover you didn't know about a particular topic as much as you thought you did."

You should always interact with people who leave you comments, even if it's just to say thank you for taking the time to read your article and sharing feedback. If it's just an insult, however, simply ignore it and move on. In fact, don't be shy about hitting the delete button on those comments. It's always best not to feed the trolls. How you respond in these moments will show others your true nature and might be what they remember you for—more than anything you wrote in your article. Make sure you think carefully before responding.

If you get hundreds of comments or even more, it might get difficult to respond to each fully. Still, do your best to acknowledge as many people as possible. Most people will appreciate the time you took to respond to them and will feel heard by you. Also, your interactions with your readers will look good to anyone who finishes reading your article. They'll be more likely to see you in a positive light and feel encouraged to leave their own comments. Lastly, it helps increase the visibility of your posts—a significant benefit.

The more you practice writing and interacting with your readers, the more you'll build your authority and credibility. As a result, you will be seen as a source of not only inspiration but also wisdom. You'll start learning what your readers care about, which will help you with your future content creation. It might take anywhere from a few weeks to a few years until writing and publishing feel natural to you. No matter what, start now. Even if your writing at the moment isn't your best, you'll still get credit for trying, and that's better than nothing.

Things to focus on in the next seven days:

1. What were your favorite topics that you liked, commented on, or shared on LinkedIn in the past 30 days? To see your activities, visit the Activity section of your profile.
2. What makes an article on LinkedIn captivating, and what posts or articles caught your attention?
3. Is there anything you've done or written as part of your student experience that you can repurpose for an article on LinkedIn?

Things to do in the next seven days:

1. Choose at least three topics you want to focus on when writing articles on LinkedIn that align with your career aspirations. Make a list of the main points you'd like to cover for each topic.
2. Create a document with top writing tips, and keep examples of the best articles you've read on LinkedIn to help guide your writing.
3. Choose at least 2-3 assignments that align with your career aspirations that you would like to share with your LinkedIn network. Look through your essays, projects, lab experiments, business ideas, etc. for inspiration.

You've done it!

You've reached the end of Part Two of this book and are now on your way to the last section. We hope you've enjoyed reading it and found these last several chapters useful in helping you see your path to success on LinkedIn. We also hope you agree we've laid out many different ways for you to find your own style and have helped you see what your own version of success on LinkedIn might look like. You now have all the essentials you'll need for this journey, and if you've started using these tips and best practices, you're well beyond what most students, graduates, and even professionals are doing on LinkedIn.

But wait—we're guessing that if you made it this far, you want to go even further. You're not the type of person who wants to do the bare minimum. Good. We wrote the next and final part of this book to help you go above and beyond the basics.

PART III:
APPLYING LINKEDIN BEYOND THE BASICS

CHAPTER 11

LINKEDIN ACTION STEPS FOR YOUR CAREER PLANNING

So far, a lot of this book has been about helping you get a job by using LinkedIn. Now, we want to start thinking a little bigger—or a lot bigger, depending on your goals and ambitions! With most people dreading going to work each day, we believe it's important you don't end up feeling that way. To make sure that doesn't happen, we want you to start designing your career plan. It isn't meant to be a highly structured plan; in fact, what you'll need is much less exact and much more meaningful.

In this chapter, we'll encourage you to start making some critical choices that will guide you, we hope, for many years to come. Some of these choices will be easier for you to make than others, but they are all equally important in creating a highly creative, resilient, and adaptable mindset necessary for achieving your career goals. You'll also set goals that are realistic yet challenging enough to push you to achieve more than you've ever thought possible. *You* get to decide how you measure your progress.

This book's purpose was never to tell you what success is, only what it might look like and what you can do to define it for yourself. Here, we'll also introduce you to a few students who have already been through this journey and whom we helped find success beyond their university lives.

You're in the final stretch now. Let's go!

The Intersection of Your Passion, Skills, and What the World Needs

Earlier in this book, we mentioned a YouTube video called "How to Find Your Passion"[15] by Jason Silva. We recommend you watch it again if you can't remember it. We've shared this video in workshops at universities to both simplify and enrich the concept of following your passion and to demonstrate how to do it in a few easy steps.

In the video, Jason asks you, the viewer, to think of fifteen topics you are curious about. Then, he asks you to find two or three overlapping areas on that list. This overlap will help you find your purpose. You'll know you found that sweet spot because of the surge of dopamine it'll give you. This euphoric feeling will inform you about the type of work you find meaningful.

Further, to find your mission, he asks you to make a list of challenges the world is facing and see which ones you can help solve, given the purpose you identified. He suggests the intersection of your purpose with the problem you can help solve will give you the most fulfilling career.

What if you still have no idea what drives you to do and be your best? We've all been there at some point. You may have so many interests that you just don't know where to start, or you might feel your interests don't have anything to do with conventional career paths. Both feelings are perfectly acceptable, but you can't use them as excuses for not pursuing your ideal career. Still early in your career, you have a great opportunity to look for any roles that align with those interests, and it's also a great time to talk about your interests so that you can get helpful advice about different opportunities you may not be considering.

Don't sabotage yourself by not taking your interests seriously. Someone somewhere is doing it, enjoying it, and getting paid for it. What are we trying to say here? Share as much as you can about your interests!

When it comes to your LinkedIn profile, do you showcase all your interests there too? Many students and graduates feel confused about it.

---

15 Jason Silva: Shots of Awe, "How to Find Your Passion," *YouTube* video, 2:11, June 7, 2016, https://www.youtube.com/watch?v=HScOL_aOMrw

They often ask us: *Should I list everything I'm interested in and I've done in my profile? Won't people think I don't know what I want and can't settle on what type of job I want to do?*

The answer is always the same: don't hide your interests and experience.

Now, more than ever, employers want to know as much as they can about your professional background. It'll help them understand what unique skills and experience you can bring to the workplace. The most innovative and progressive companies in the world celebrate their diversity, and few, if any, are looking for only one type of employee. Don't limit yourself when you're still standing on the starting line.

What do you really love to do? What are you really good at? How can this help other people, and is that help valuable enough that it could pay your bills and support your lifestyle? How easy or how difficult would it be for you to pursue your passion and apply it to your career? Would you have to make any sacrifices at first to get started? What's holding you back?

Ask yourself these questions, and answer them as truthfully as you can. Then, look through your LinkedIn connections for people who are passionate, highly skilled, and solving important problems. One great place to look is the recommendations on their profiles. What do others say about them?

Start reaching out to those people, and start building strong relationships with them. If you've already connected with them, start talking to them and getting their help. The good news is you'll find that usually these positive and passionate individuals are more than happy to help others. We're not asking you to go after CEOs or elected officials. But do look for anyone at any level who you think can help you talk through your passion, skills, and best ways to apply them. We find that the most exciting careers rarely have only one or a few paths you can follow.

It seems the concept of following one's passion is treated with caution these days. More and more people think that telling young people and experienced professionals to pursue their passions is a bad idea. You might think the same way. What if what you love doing is just a hobby? What if your passion can't pay your bills and support the lifestyle you want? What if your passion convinces you to leave a good job and take too many risks?

These questions are all fair, but they miss an important point. It's not your passion that gets you in trouble. It's not knowing and accepting what your passion means to your life and career that can lead to feelings of failure and disappointment. If you are passionate about doing social work or working for non profits but you also want to earn like an investment banker, you're not really understanding and accepting what your passion means to you.

Finding and following your passion isn't the secret to happiness or career success. If you speak to enough people who have been on this journey, you will hear how much many of them struggled at the beginning of their careers. Most people choose the safe path and settle for reliable paychecks and benefits even if they dislike or even hate their jobs. Others can't bear the 9-5 grind, painful office politics, and awful managers.

What feels right to you? Only you can answer that. Don't let others define that for you, but be open and willing to listen to their ideas, applying what makes sense to your life and work. Maybe you do need to have an "okay" or "normal" job so you can continue searching for your passion, or perhaps you can accept to live a frugal life so you can do what you really love and eventually turn it into a successful business. It is a personal decision for everyone.

When you reach out to your LinkedIn connections, ask them questions that can reveal why they chose their professions, how they measure their successes, how they overcame their failures, what it's like to work in their companies, and what they enjoy the most about their careers. The answers will reveal not only details about their jobs but also the kind of person they are and the kind of life they live—and that's what really matters.

Your Goals and Success Metrics

As a student, you might have pretty straightforward goals. They might be as simple as making sure you get good grades, pass your exams, and graduate with a degree that will help you succeed after university. Perhaps your goal is to start a business and find entrepreneurial opportunities during and after university. Or maybe you've decided university isn't for you and you'd like to find a temporary job while pursuing other interests.

No matter what your plan is, we want to help you start thinking about ways that LinkedIn could help you achieve your career goals. We also want to help you pick milestones to celebrate each step in your journey to keep you going through the inevitable highs and lows you'll encounter in pursuit of your dream career.

You can separate your LinkedIn development goals into four main categories:

1. Development of self: Do you have a stellar professional brand attracting the right people?
2. Development of search: Are you searching holistically and effectively enough to uncover a vast variety of relevant and exciting roles?
3. Development of relationships: Have you built relationships with hundreds of professionals representing the jobs and careers you're looking for?
4. Development of engagement: Do you share interesting content and engage with your network in a way that makes you memorable?

What does success look like in each of these categories? Here are some ways to think about this:

Look at how many people are viewing your profile—are you getting a few dozen views a month or hundreds? The higher the number of people who can find you, the higher your chances of being discovered by the right people for the right opportunities will be. Then, you have to make sure they actually click through and scroll through your profile because you sound like an amazing person and professional!

How many skills have you listed, and how many people have endorsed you? The more skills you have, the more chances of being endorsed you'll have, demonstrating you have all or most of the required skills for the jobs you're applying for. If you don't have many endorsements, ask people whom you've worked with to provide you with endorsements on a few of your skills.

How many recommendations have you asked for, and how many do

you have on your profile? As we said before, this is a critical area of your profile—one you can't afford to overlook. Do you have at least three great recommendations from respected individuals and leaders? Do these recommendations specifically cover your unique strengths, contributions, and achievements based on each job or project you've done?

Finally, are you following people and organizations in your desired industry? If an industry professional visits your profile, will they get the impression that you care about what's happening in that industry? Remember that people can see your activity and publications on your profile. Your articles, status updates, and posts you've liked, commented on, or shared will appear in that section. You want to make sure that what people see there reflects the kind of professional you said you were in your profile.

When assessing the appropriateness of your LinkedIn activities, here is a good rule to follow: you should be 100% confident and comfortable discussing anything in your activity section during an interview or professional meeting. You never know what a recruiter or hiring manager might pick from your profile to ask you about during the interview.

Your 3-Month Strategy: 30, 60, 90 Days

Let's say you followed all our advice so far, and you feel you have a good grasp of the LinkedIn fundamentals. You're now looking for those career opportunities, wondering when you'll see the results from all your hard work. If that describes you, you need to have a LinkedIn strategy you can commit to for at least a month, but preferably three months, as we've suggested with the title of this book.

Month One

Spend each day choosing different organizations relevant to the career you'd like to pursue. Don't worry about how big or small and how well-known or unknown the organizations are. Focus on one industry for now.

1. Spend one hour looking through all the jobs available in each organization. See if you notice anything interesting in each type of role.

Take a piece of paper, and on one side, write down positions that sound like a good fit. On the other side, list any interesting positions you hadn't considered before related to what you'd like to do. Don't avoid listing jobs because you don't feel you have all the right skills, work experience, or education. This isn't the time to limit yourself!

2. Prioritize both lists based on the roles that most excite you, based on the information you have now. Have a list of at least 20 jobs in total.

3. Prioritize both lists based on the roles that are a good fit based on your skills, work experience, seniority level, and education. Make sure you read the preferred and minimum requirements carefully to be able to apply for the role. The fewer requirements you meet, the lower that job should be on your list.

4. Prioritize both lists by the number of available jobs you're finding for each role in your desired region. Notice that the same types of roles might have slightly different job titles in different companies.

5. Now, look at your first list. Which roles from that list also appear at the top of all three categories? You might go with the top two to five that appear highest in all three categories, indicating a higher chance of getting interviews and being eventually hired.

6. Make sure to have a good summary and description of each role so you start getting used to the language the organizations use to describe the jobs you'll be applying for.

    Note: This is valuable information. Consider using the same terminology in your profile.

7. Whether it's on your desk or your wall, keep these lists where you can see them so they can remind you of your targets every day.

Month Two

After the first month, start focusing on finding people who might be able to help you in those organizations. Spend each day finding employees working in the same offices, departments, and teams as the people occupying the roles you found in the first month.

Don't limit your search to employees who have the exact or similar titles to the roles on your list. It is, of course, beneficial to connect and speak with them, but at this point, you want to create a large pool of people who might be able to give you useful information.

1. Spend one hour each day looking through the profiles of these employees to decide which ones might be the best to approach for more information. Consider how complete their profiles are, how active they are on LinkedIn, and whether they share any interesting content about their work and industry. You want to prioritize these individuals as they tend to be more likely to respond and more likely to offer you something useful.

2. Aim to compile a list of 20 employees from each organization. This number could vary, depending on the size of the companies, but we encourage you to go for as many as you can.

3. Spend each day sending as many connection requests and messages as you can to the people on your list to let them know about the roles you're considering and the questions you have about those roles. After you've had a dialogue with them, ask them to introduce you to others if they're not the best person to help you. If the initial interactions go well, ask to have a quick call with them to learn more about the role and the company they work for. See if you can get in touch with the right recruiters, hiring managers, and other decision-makers.

4. Don't send the exact same message to 20 employees in the same company. This will be considered spam, and you'll look unprofessional if they ever talk to each other about your message. Each one should be highly personalized and should ask relevant questions the recipient is likely to answer based on their role and responsibilities.

5. Try to send 30-40 connection requests and messages throughout this month, increasing your chances of getting good responses. If you're really ambitious, try to hit 100—that's just three to four a day for a month. It doesn't sound too difficult when you think about it in these terms.

Ultimately, you want to get referred for the roles highest on your list so you have a much better chance of getting at least an interview. However, don't panic if you can't get any referrals at this point.

Month Three

Our hope is that by this point, you've secured some interviews for a few of these roles, or at least you're calling and meeting some of the people on your lists. We know this part can be incredibly daunting. Don't be too hard on yourself if you still don't feel comfortable approaching people. Take small steps each month, and you'll notice you'll get more comfortable with time.

Here are further steps you need to take to advance your career-building plan.

1. If you've made a lot of new connections and received a lot of responses, you might forget to respond to some people. Review your messages, and make a list of these people. It doesn't look good if you don't respond to someone who has taken the time to help you. Don't make a bad impression that can affect your chances of getting a job before you even walk through the door. You never know who talks to whom or has influence over someone making hiring decisions.

2. Make sure you're ready and well-organized for each call or meeting, whether the person makes hiring decisions or not. During phone calls, be somewhere quiet and with great Wi-Fi if you are doing a video call. Have a notebook with a list of reminders about the person (name, role, interesting facts) and questions. You'll demonstrate you respect the other person's time by keeping the conversation productive. Stick to what you agreed to discuss. Make sure you understand whether the call or meeting is part of the interviewing process or an informational chat. Don't make assumptions about these calls, and ask for clarity if you're ever unclear about the hiring process.

3. If you've made it to the interviewing stage, make sure you always know who'll be in the room, and research them as much as you can. Don't be afraid to mention you've talked to other employees in the company, sharing what you've learned from them. Focus on what

you enjoyed about these conversations. Also talk about the challenges you uncovered that would be well-served by your unique set of skills, experience, and education. Most hiring managers will be impressed by the amount of work you've done to get this far. They'll appreciate the fact that you have more knowledge about the position and the company than most candidates would ever bother to gather.

4. Finally, don't assume that the people interviewing you know everything about you from your profile. Some may still rely on a copy of your CV on the day of the interview, so do everything you can to expand on every single item beyond the sheet of paper in front of them. After the interview, reach out to them again on LinkedIn to thank them for their time, summarize key points from the meeting, and reiterate why you think you're the right person for the role.

You can do much more than what we've listed in this 90-day strategy, but this should give you enough to take more advanced steps toward the beginning of a great career. With this strategy, you should be able to see how much time and effort it can take to get worthwhile results on LinkedIn. Finding and applying for jobs on LinkedIn is incredibly simple, while building your future career takes real guts and effort. Don't let yourself forget that on this incredible journey of highs and lows.

Real Students, Real Stories

Over the years, we've worked with thousands of students, staff, and faculty from many different colleges, universities, and business schools. Most of the people we work with have used LinkedIn in some way or another, but some continue to tell us they're not comfortable and haven't seen much value from using it. If you are not getting value from it, look at how you can change your approach to it.

This is why several years ago we started running workshops at well-known universities in North America and the UK. We realized that although most universities provided some guidance on the use of LinkedIn, they didn't have real experts, meaningful content, or a structured approach to it. After attending several sessions at different universities, we were shocked to see slides containing outdated images of LinkedIn and incorrect advice showing students how to copy and paste their resumes into their LinkedIn profiles—with little mention of anything else.

We knew then that the speakers and organizers had never really used LinkedIn other than to create a profile, while students were left thinking the platform wasn't that useful to them or exciting. It might sound dramatic, but Miguel was so upset that he decided to create the first "LinkedIn for Students" program in the UK. Thankfully, he found a university that was willing to offer the program as a six-week pilot to its students. That's right, six weeks of LinkedIn curriculum, dedicated to taking students from knowing zero about LinkedIn to navigating it like a pro! That was also when we decided to write this book.

Miguel tells this story to illustrate the success of such workshops.

"Back in 2016, a young single mother attended one of my workshops in London. She was struggling to find work after years of unemployment. With three young children, it was nearly impossible for her to focus on her career. She had decided to pursue further education and added additional degrees to her credentials, but it seemed it wasn't enough to get her the job she wanted.

I encouraged this young mother to start looking for other women on LinkedIn who were also busy mothers who had taken career breaks at some point in their lives. She began to realize there were plenty of women who weren't afraid to share their stories of struggle and creative ways to find success on their own terms. Among other things, they talked about career transitions, setting up businesses, or choosing employers who allowed them flexible working options. Suddenly, this young mother had dozens of examples of ways to move forward. Sometimes, the best thing LinkedIn can do for you is help you find people who have overcome some of the same problems you're facing.

During this time, I was also helping a young man who had recently moved to the UK from China, finding the transition difficult. While his university offered services to support international students, he didn't feel they were supportive enough. Many students felt the same way. One of the things I admired about this student was his passion for science and biology. While he had no professional experience, he shared with me all the things he did in his personal time to continue his research inside and outside the lab at his university.

His LinkedIn profile, however, had none of that extra information. It portrayed him only as an undergraduate student studying biochemistry. I realized that his negative perception of the UK and his university was preventing him from sharing his passion and from finding ways to promote himself. After a few months of encouraging him to look through the profiles of other scientists and company pages of pharmaceutical companies, I saw his perception of what he could achieve by using LinkedIn changed entirely.

Soon, his profile was filled with information about his work and ways it could change the way we treat age-related health issues. A year after the workshops, he found a variety of lab assistant internships in the field he was most passionate about.

These students showed us that LinkedIn didn't just help them find career opportunities, but, more importantly, it enabled them to see themselves differently—not just as a struggling unemployed single mother or a disadvantaged student in a foreign country."

How Successful Students Went Beyond the Basics

If you were to see the profiles of the most successful students on LinkedIn, you would never guess they were students until you looked at their education sections. While most students use their profile headlines to tell the world where and what they study, the most ambitious students show the world what they're passionate about and how they help others.

The world of work is increasingly moving away from education-based requirements for jobs. Companies have realized hiring someone with a university degree doesn't mean the person will become a successful long-term employee. We're not telling you this because we don't believe in higher education. We tell you this to help you understand the mindsets of most organizations.

That's why on LinkedIn, you need to go beyond the basics of a student profile. From now on, you need to remind yourself you're not only a student but also a driven, passionate, and professional individual with the skills, experience, and motivation to achieve more in life. The people who will consider hiring you will want to know how you went above and beyond the life and responsibilities of a student. You should be proud of any academic achievements, but we suggest you lead with professional results from any projects, internships, work-study, volunteer experience, or part-time work you've done. Give an overview and the responsibilities of the job, but focus on your unique contributions, problems you solved, and value you delivered.

If you're struggling to come up with professional experience to add to your profile, we suggest you look for short-term work you could offer to others. For example, if you're good at writing or graphic design, could you provide your services on a freelancing website? Could you reach out to a small business or a startup to see what help they need?

If you've got your daily essentials covered as a student and this is the first time you're doing freelance work, don't worry about how much you are getting paid, if at all. If you've got the skills and time to do this, do it for the experience and recommendations, which will eventually lead to the referrals you are after.

Each time you start and end a project, update your work experience section of your LinkedIn profile. In between, post regular updates of your work. Always seek your client's permission to share publicly the work you do for them.

Ask for those recommendations and testimonials for your profile, website, and marketing materials. Then, ask every happy client if they're willing to refer you to others so that you can continue finding more work. Eventually, you'll get the practice and reputation you need to get paid fairly for your efforts. Who knows, you may even decide to turn your side gigs into full-time work.

If freelancing isn't your style, start looking for a part-time job. Does your school have any open positions? Perhaps they're looking for students for office assistance, event support, or other administrative assistant roles? What about the surrounding neighborhood and community? Are there any community centers, libraries, shops, restaurants, or parks offering entry-level part-time work?

Choose the hours and location that will suit your schedule so you can work comfortably. Just don't expect to be too comfortable as any work will surely stretch you, which is precisely what you want! Don't let pride get in the way of accepting a perfectly good job while you're a student. A good employer will want to see the variety of skills and experiences you bring and won't judge you because you were serving food, sweeping floors, or selling shoes while you were a student. They'll be glad to see you spent time in the workplace and not just in the classroom.

Most universities today offer career services helping students get internships, and many require that students gain some work experience before they graduate. Students have fewer and fewer excuses not to take advantage of these professional opportunities. We understand, however, that sometimes life gets in the way and you may find yourself at the end of your student journey without the professional experience you need to attract the right employers. You may have a higher hill to climb, but LinkedIn can still be your best friend.

Search LinkedIn for graduate-level positions to see what they're asking for, but don't apply yet. Use filters to narrow your job search to temporary, part-time, contract, internship or volunteer positions and picking entry-level experience if you're just getting started.

Make sure you fully research these requirements to understand the profiles of candidates these organizations are looking for. Notice the types of words, responsibilities, tools, skills, and other requirements listed in the job descriptions. Does your LinkedIn profile use similar language? And does it quickly and effectively show the potential employer you're the right fit for the role?

Now, take a look at the profiles of the people in that business. Note what the company has been sharing recently on LinkedIn and other social media channels. Connect with them, and follow them, using best practices described in this book.

Next, start sharing content on LinkedIn related to the role and the type of work the business does. Do this, whether it takes a few days or a few weeks, until you feel that anyone looking at your profile from that company would be impressed by your knowledge and motivation. You may not have all the experience they're looking for, but they'll quickly see you have just the right attitude for the job and are hungry to learn and achieve more.

This is how the best students and graduates on LinkedIn think and operate. They think of themselves as more than just students. They search for an opportunity to learn beyond their coursework, and they understand that employers today care more about the time you spend in the workplace than the time you spend in the classroom. All this is reflected in their profiles and activities on LinkedIn in simple but powerful ways.

How You Can Get Work Experience While Studying

Getting work experience while you're busy writing essays, studying for exams, and having fun may feel overwhelming to you. You're probably also not thrilled that you have to give up some of your free time, whether it's to relax on your own or go out with friends, to start building your career. It's perfectly fine to feel that way. You don't want any one thing to dominate your life and cause you unnecessary stress.

On the other hand, you likely hope to see good results from all the time, money, and effort you invested while at university. Not having the career you want once you graduate can negatively affect you much more—and for much longer—than any drawbacks of working while in school can.

Go through your calendar to see what free time you have. Pick time slots when you can do the activities described in this chapter. Perhaps you have a day when you don't have many classes, or you decide that Sunday mornings or afternoons will be your professional development days. Whatever you decide, keep yourself accountable to your commitment so you can stick with it. It might help to share your plan with a friend, inviting them to try something similar so you can keep each other going.

The seemingly small step of making professional development as part of your student life is in fact a big leap toward preparing you for your future career. No one will do it for you. You have to take ownership of your time outside of your coursework and decide to sacrifice small chunks of it so that you can increase your chances of career success after graduation. Don't expect your degree and your grades to do all the talking for you.

Go to your university page on LinkedIn, and look for alumni. Start with those who have recently graduated, and see what they're currently doing. Don't be too rigid in considering only those who have a similar background or studied the same subject as you. Challenge yourself to choose professionals who differ from you, e.g., those who have roles and work for companies you would never consider. What you discover might be just as useful or even more useful than what you'd find out from people similar to you.

This is an opportunity to search far and wide for anyone who can share with you what they did during their student years and after graduation to get the jobs they wanted. See if these diverse professionals can provide insights into any projects, internships, or part-time work they did as students and how they managed to do it in addition to their student responsibilities. Find out if they were able to use any of this experience as a springboard to their current roles or if they even turned their internships or side gigs into full-time work. This isn't about getting all the secrets to success you can replicate—it is about finding inspiration for what's possible.

The World of Work Today and in the Future

You've probably encountered many different stories, articles, films, and TV shows about utopian as well as dystopian visions of the future. For a long time, it seemed such extremes belonged only to the world of fiction, but if you think about the last decade, much of what many would have thought belonged to the world of fiction has now become our reality.

Whether we look at technology, politics, or society in general, we see some shocking developments few, if any, could have predicted. The pace of transformation in the world of work has been staggering, and yet the pace of change to prepare people to face this new world has been slow.

A PricewaterhouseCoopers study "Workforce of the Future: The Competing Forces Shaping 2030"[16] reported the following statistics:

- 37% of people say they are worried about automation putting jobs at risk
- 74% are ready to learn new skills or re-train to remain employable in the future
- 60% think "few people will have stable, long-term employment in the future"
- 73% think technology can never replace the human mind.

This report presents four different scenarios when it comes to the world of work, assigning each a different color: red, blue, green, and yellow.

The red world is where innovation flourishes and the world is ruled by digital platforms, online services, and technology of all shapes and sizes. Large corporations and highly skilled employees benefit from it, but their success comes at a cost to others. Many workers are left out of this labor market without the needed skills, and regulation is unable to control the pace of change affecting the lives of millions.

In the blue world, capitalism reigns supreme, and organizations protect their size and power to maximize their profits, pushing out and eliminating smaller competitors. The focus is on identifying and catering to individual preferences rather than being socially responsible.

In the green world, the focus is on corporate responsibility, social conscience, and environmentally friendly practices. Business thinks beyond maximizing profits and understands it has a responsibility to protect the wellbeing of humans and the planet. Employees increasingly demand that the work they do has a positive impact on society and that their companies' values reflect their own.

In the yellow world, humans come first. Employees and companies search for a greater sense of meaning, belonging, and purpose with the

---

16 PricewaterhouseCoopers, "Workforce of the Future: The Competing Forces Shaping 2030," https://www.pwc.com/gx/en/services/people-organisation/publications/workforce-of-the-future.html

products they create and services they deliver. Artisans, artists, and other creatives thrive in this world where the human approach is highly valued.

Today, if you look across different regions, industries, and organizations, you can find elements of all these worlds. The question for you is not how to prepare for one potential future over another, but how to prepare for all of them. Your challenge is to make sure that who you are and whom you want to become is aligned with what you choose to pursue and the kind of world you decide to help build.

You will need to become highly adaptable and willing to accept that your future employment will depend on learning much more than you could ever learn during all your years of formal education. Just consider how much things have changed since your primary school years, and the world keeps changing at an accelerated pace.

Published on the website The Muse, citing other studies, an infographic titled "10 Shocking Stats About Employee Engagement,"[17] states that 70% of US workers are not engaged at work and 75% of employees who quit their jobs leave because of their bosses.

You've probably heard many other examples of people choosing jobs that make them unhappy and unhealthy. The sad truth is that even with all the data and stories, employers still fail to grasp the underlying reasons for employee disengagement. When they do take actions, most actions fail to make a difference or, in extreme cases, backfire and make things much worse.

Unfortunately, many of your career choices will lead you to disengaged workplaces. The numbers tell us that. To avoid this trap, you can steer your career in the right direction early on. When considering working for an organization, do everything you can to quickly uncover its culture, values, work style preferences, and expectations. Don't hold back—research in full, and ask as many questions as you can. Ask what people love and what they don't like about their jobs. That simple question may reveal the key information you need to help you make the most important decision of your career.

---

17 Catherine Jessen, "10 Shocking Stats About Employee Engagement," *The Muse*, https://www.themuse.com/advice/10-shocking-stats-about-employee-engagement

A great way to improve your chances of finding a great place to work at is to ask about the company's onboarding, or induction, process:

- How do they welcome new employees?
- What are the first week and first few months like?
- Do they provide formal training to help you become more familiar with your tasks?

These questions will reveal not only whether the company has a good way of onboarding new employees but also what success will look like in your first few months—the most critical time for a new employee. According to a Gallup report[18], only 12% of employees strongly agree their organization does a good job of onboarding. This further proves why maintaining employee engagement in the long term is such a hard thing to achieve for the vast majority of companies.

Any recruiter or hiring manager who struggles to answer this question or dismisses the importance of this initial period for a new employee deserves a red flag in our book. No matter the size of the company or your role, you should expect some sort of preparation for your first couple of weeks at a minimum. A really great company will make sure to provide you with the training and resources needed for you to become as self-sufficient as possible in the first few months of your job. They'll also schedule time for you to meet your team and other people in the office you'll be working with closely.

That being said, don't expect every company to roll out the red carpet for you when you arrive. You might be joining a perfectly good company with a small team and few resources to provide formal training. In these cases, you should still expect a bare minimum of support from your manager or other team members to help you get started. Don't be afraid to speak up and ask for help if you're not getting what you need. Be proactive, and find as many ways to learn as you can.

---

18 Ryan Pendell and Jim Harter, "10 Gallup Reports to Share with Your Leaders in 2019," *Gallup*, January 4, 2019, https://www.gallup.com/workplace/245786/gallup-reports-share-leaders-2019.aspx

Finding a highly engaged workplace is getting easier than ever thanks to LinkedIn. You no longer have to depend on the word of job advertisers or recruiters. Now, you can go directly to the sources of knowledge throughout the company—the employees themselves. That said, make sure to ask the onboarding question, and listen carefully to the answers. Your wellbeing and happiness at work depend on it.

Put Your University Investment to Good Use

If you're at a university today, the most important thing you need to ask yourself is how you'll make the most of the investment you've already made (and plan to continue making). What will your time, effort, and money help you achieve? As we've been saying in this book, your transformation from a student to a professional must happen before you graduate or soon after. That means you need to think critically about each step you take in your university career and ways to translate each one of those into your professional development.

Every class, assignment, and exam needs to become much more than a simple benchmark to measure your suitability to advance to the next academic year and eventually to get a finished degree. You are now the type of student who looks at your academic activities as opportunities to question what you learn from lectures, share your work with your professional network, and challenge yourself beyond academic standards and expectations.

Rarely will any of us have a better opportunity to develop ourselves without the worries of raising a family, paying the bills, and working a full-time job. Your time at university is a golden time to maximize your professional development and transform your life. So many of us look back at our university years with blissful nostalgia, reminding ourselves of all the fun times and the very few responsibilities we had. There's nothing wrong with those happy memories, except for the fact that most of us didn't take full advantage of our student years to grow professionally and define our paths to success.

After graduation, many of us spend years, if not decades, bouncing from job to job without a clear direction. Or we settle for something that doesn't match our passions. We hope by reading this book and using LinkedIn like a pro, you've decided to take a different path and jumpstart a successful career.

Use Your Community to Succeed

The title of this chapter includes the words *action steps*, and we meant them literally. At some point, you will have to leave your comfort zone behind and take actual steps in the real world. You are surrounded by opportunities every day to connect and learn from others, and we don't just mean at school or in the workplace. There are clubs, groups, events, meetups, campaigns, and organizations of all shapes and sizes surrounding you. Whether you live in a big city or a small town, the opportunities are there, and you have no excuse not to take advantage of them.

Look around to see what types of businesses operate in your area. Do any of them represent industries you're interested in? Can you find these companies on LinkedIn? Can you see which employees might be worth meeting? Challenge yourself to connect with the people who work in your community.

Start with anyone who is within walking distance or a short drive away. Even if you're not looking for work, be on the lookout for any of these businesses that are hiring. If the role sounds interesting, reach out with a list of questions, letting the hiring manager know you just seek more information. Every call you make and every meeting you organize will prepare you well for the years ahead when you're applying for jobs and demonstrating your skills during the hiring process. Don't over-rely on emails.

Try to find a calendar of events or meetups happening around your community. Search online for topics, products, or services you enjoy, and see what's nearby. Identify communities across social media related to your interests, and reach out to members in the group you identify with. Find out if these communities hold events that bring members together at a specific location.

Don't downplay your interests or underestimate the power of building relationships in the real world. Nothing can make a difference in your career and professional success as meeting and learning from the right people can. Don't forget to use the LinkedIn app on your phone to research new connections and connect on the go. Now if your family, friends, or teachers ever give you a hard time for being on your phone while you're using LinkedIn like a pro, you don't have to feel too guilty!

The Ultimate Student and Graduate Assessments

In this book, we've talked a lot about LinkedIn because we believe it's one of the most powerful online platforms for students, graduates, and educators. Any kind of meaningful success, however, depends on many different factors working together. That's why we also want you to have full awareness of some key aspects of your life that will ultimately define how you feel about yourself and what you need to do to keep learning and growing. The following assessment will help you do that.

We know different people value different things in life, so use this assessment however you wish, but do consider each area carefully, thinking about what it means to your life and career.

Rate yourself from 1-10 (1 = Extremely Low, 10 = Extremely High) on the following:

I take good care of myself: Make sure you feel physically and emotionally prepared to deal with whatever life throws at you. We won't presume to tell you what you should eat, how much exercise you should get, or how many pounds you should shed. You probably already feel pressure to hit some targets, and it's great if that's what you're aiming for. Just make sure you take care of your whole self, not just your physical image, so that you can feel and do your best. Look across LinkedIn—you'll see success has many looks and versions.

I dedicate time to my family: It's important to show love and appreciation to our family members, even when they annoy and frustrate us. Don't forget the whole picture beyond the current frame in which you're viewing your family members. Remember, there is a lot of history before this moment, and there is a lot of unknown future ahead of you. You never know when you'll need someone who loves you unconditionally and how long you'll have them in your life.

I have friends that bring out the best in me: A lot of who we are and what we do is influenced by the people we spend the most time with. Creating and nurturing friendships is an indispensable part of a well-lived life. The best of friends can be both our biggest advocates and harshest critics. They support us emotionally when we struggle but aren't afraid to tell us when they think we're wrong. Whether you can count your best friends on one hand or have dozens of them, it's important to consider how they influence you. Spend time with the ones who build you up to be a better person, and let go of the ones dragging you down.

My life has a purpose: Everyone seeks purpose in their lives, but it's okay to feel lost from time to time. Being young or being a student doesn't mean you don't have a mission or purpose in life. What type of work would get you excited? What have you done for others that has made you feel proud about yourself? In what situations were you able to add real value? Everyone has these experiences, whether small or significant, and we can all imagine what our purpose in life is even if we haven't had the chance to fully experience it. Fast-forward to the end of your life and look back. What would be some of the most meaningful things you've accomplished for yourself and others? Go on the journey, and meet the people most likely to help you find it.

I'm waiting/searching for the right partner, or I'm in a healthy relationship: There's nothing like the simple and complex feeling of love. We're wired with this incredible emotional response that can ultimately lead us to make one of the most, if not *the* most, important decision of our lives: whom we spend our lives with. Few things can have as much of an impact on our success, happiness, and overall wellbeing as our chosen partner in life.

Do what you need to find the right one for you. Be willing to see beyond the surface—that changes anyway. Much like a good friend, a good partner brings out the best in you and makes you feel your best in a way that no one else can. But even the best ones aren't without their flaws, just like you. Be willing to forgive if being together is worth the bumps in the road. Don't accept mistreatment, and don't let feelings of inadequacy weigh you down. Be transparent and communicate. Find compromises, and be open to differences if it means you make a better team.

At the same time, don't be afraid of or be too hard on yourself for being single if you're not quite ready or haven't found the right person yet. No one should pressure you into it. Take your time. Don't use just your heart when taking this big step; use your mind. The best partners will respect and support who you are and what you want to do with your life and expect the same from you. Get it right, and you'll both take each other to new heights, no matter the storms you'll have to overcome to get there.

I spend on experiences that enrich my life: When we say spending, we don't mean just money. Are you investing time and energy in things you love to do? It's as simple as that. You shouldn't be spending all your waking hours studying and working. Some superhumans can live like this, but it usually comes at huge costs and personal sacrifices that most of us wouldn't be willing to make.

Make time to be alone, and treat yourself to things that delight you. They don't have to be expensive. Go on that walk or run while you listen to your playlists, podcasts, or audiobooks. Join a gym or dancing class. Find a cheap, short flight to a new destination you've always wanted to visit, even if it's just for a few days. Plan a nice dinner at your home, and invite your friends. Or go out to a food market and shop for ingredients to cook a meal together. Go to a salon to do your hair and makeup, or get a facial and massage every once in a while. Play your favorite sports and games. Go to a live concert, symphony, or opera. Shop for one outfit that truly brings you joy. Make time for your hobbies. A pleasurable and rewarding hobby can be a great way to de-stress.

Find others who share your interests, and enjoy the time you spend together whether it costs you nothing or takes a pretty penny. These days, you can find plenty of ways to find the best deals or even free activities in your community. None of this is asking you to ignore your responsibilities and avoid hard work the rest of the time. Simply spend wisely on the experiences that matter to you.

I look for ways to learn from every situation: Every once in awhile, even when you feel you're doing everything right, things don't go your way. That's a fact of life, right? However, it's not life that needs to make sense; it's your approach to it. What's important is what you take from every situation, good or bad.

Focus on what you can learn from the experience and how you can get better at facing the next one. Don't let your mistakes or failures define you. You are in control of your emotions, not the other way around. Resilience is an amazing skill to develop in your life and career. It allows you to get back up and stand firmly against adversity. Reflecting on your reactions to difficult times will teach you about yourself and show you ways to approach things differently in the future.

At the same time, seek help and advice from others so you can gain different perspectives. Listen to constructive feedback without becoming defensive. Remember that you're here to learn from every situation. Learning about what you don't agree with or believe in is just as important as what you do agree with and believe in. When you open yourself up to learning from every situation, you open yourself up to challenging everything you think of yourself and others. We truly feel that's what the world needs right now.

HelloGrads in the UK

To support you in your life after university, we recommend you visit the www.hellograds.com website. It is a knowledge and support base for nearly every aspect of post-university life. Below are some great student and graduate tips from the website.

Career Tips for Students (from HelloGrads)

While you're at university, think of yourself not just as a student but as a budding professional. In addition to making a start with LinkedIn (as thoroughly explained in this book), you can do plenty of other things to prepare for graduation and ease yourself into working life.

Use Your Facilities

At university, you have access to a huge array of facilities to help your portfolio pop and your CV sing. Take advantage of them! Borrow a decent camera and get someone to take a good professional headshot for your LinkedIn profile. Use a studio to make your final projects pop, print and bind the essay you're most proud of to take to interviews, and learn to build a website.

Contacts

You're surrounded by lecturers and staff members who may be very helpful to you in the future. In addition to teaching you, a lot of university staff are doing research projects or working/have worked in your industry. Connect with them on LinkedIn, chat with them about the direction you might want to take, or ask them for ideas! The point is, they form a significant part of your education, and they can be very helpful in guiding you beyond this, but you have to make the first move. This is an important step to building your network—starting with people who know you.

Work Hard, Play Hard

Use your long holidays to get in some work experience, internships, or work shadowing days to get a taste of working life and check whether you're suited to the areas you're interested in. It's a great chance to try things without the time pressure or financial consequence you will have once you graduate. Mix this up, however, with other fun non-work-related activities—once you start working, you won't get a three-month summer holiday!

Join Clubs and Societies

Apart from the fact it should be fun and is a great way to meet other people, joining a club can set you apart when you're applying for jobs. It's an interest to talk about in interviews, and it can teach you some valuable life skills such as teamwork, dealing with third parties, working to deadlines or within budgets, and leading projects.

Prep Your CV

If you haven't already written your CV, get a head start so you can be ready when you begin applying for jobs. Start by setting up the layout and noting some achievements and any work experience you already have. Then your CV is ready to be updated or tailored to companies, and you can avoid a mad scramble before sending off an application.

Don't Forget Why You're Here

These days, simply having a degree won't make you stand out, but a good degree can improve your chances of being shortlisted for interviews and arm you with a wealth of knowledge that can come in handy at work and life in general. Go the extra mile—work hard, ask questions, use your contacts, and make this happen.

Career Tips for Graduates (from HelloGrads)

As a recent graduate, you are likely feeling a mix of emotions at the moment as you are also dealing with friends and family giving you well-intended but often ill-fitting advice about your life. We've gathered our top tips to help you through these challenging times.

Start Today

Taking charge of your life is empowering. Feeling as if you have no control is stressful. Be proactive, and start today.

Have a Plan and Stick to It

As you already know, job searching is time-consuming, and after rejections, it can be frustrating. Of course, it will need to be your main focus. Create a routine that includes fun, relaxation, exercise, and socializing. Make sure you stick to that plan—the enjoyable elements will help avoid stress, putting you in a better frame of mind to tackle the heavy stuff, such as job applications and money issues.

Take Control and Focus on Small Goals

If you find yourself saying, "I'm going to sort my life out" …no, you're not. You'll need to set small goals and smash one at a time. Update your CV, open a graduate bank account, register on the electoral roll, sort your social media profile, join a gym/choir/ team… whatever floats your boat. We all love crossing things off the to-do list, right? Reward yourself as you go, and remember that it is all progress.

Sort Your Finances

You'll need to fully understand your student loan, for starters. It's important to get to grips with money matters; good planning now will prevent money worries later. Grasp the essentials (e.g., budgeting, interest, and banking) so you can make informed decisions.

Here are a few pointers to set you in the right direction:

- The first step in taking control of your finances is to set up a budget. Budgeting isn't just about making sacrifices; it's to help you organise your money so you make sure you're living within your means and avoid building up debt.
- Don't stress over your student loan. Repayments are linked to earnings, and you don't need to start repaying until you're earning £25,000+ a year as of 2019 (UK only). Whatever your circumstances and wherever you live, make sure to get information about your student loan so you fully understand your responsibilities for repayment.
- Switch your student bank account to a graduate account. This is a minor move that could give you introductory perks and preferential terms for up to three years after graduation.

Most graduate accounts offer an interest-free overdraft, which can help you start reducing university debt. Find out how to choose the bank account that's right for you. This could be different where you live, so do your banking research to see the best options for a recent graduate.

Update Your CV/Resume

You need to be ready for any opportunity that comes your way, so prepare your CV/resume. Then tailor it to each job application to demonstrate you're the ideal candidate for the role.

This doesn't mean making things up, of course—be truthful, but choose how and what you talk about to paint the best picture of yourself. Do your research to find out what the employer is really looking for, and then adapt your CV to emphasize relevant experience, skills, and attributes best showing how you meet the job requirements and would fit in with the company culture.

Do What You Love

This is the one piece of career advice we've heard and read over and over again. We spend far too long at work not to enjoy it, and if you love what you do, you're far, far more likely to be successful at it. But there are two takes on this theme: do what you love... or love what you do.

Do what love!

> *"Do something you're very passionate about. And don't try to chase what is the hot passion of the day."*
>
> - Jeff Bezos,
> Founder of Amazon

Love what you do!

> *"Your work is going to fill a large part of your life, and the only way to be truly satisfied is to do what you believe is great work. And the only way to do great work is to love what you do."*
>
> - Steve Jobs,
> Co-founder of Apple

You might be lucky enough to have a passion for something that could earn you a decent living—numbers, developing apps, or sustainability. But if what you love doing is less lucrative (sadly, few of us can turn our favorite sports/arts/hobbies into careers), you might have to opt for something else! So, if you can't do what you love, can you love what you do?

The takeaway from this is to go into an area you find enjoyable, inspiring, or genuinely interesting. You're much more likely to grow to love what you're doing and make a success of it. Don't be seduced into a job just because it sounds impressive, fits what you think you ought to be doing, or satisfies family expectations. Follow your own path, and pursue what feels right for you. If you stop feeling drawn to it, it might be time to move on.

Do the Dreaded "Networking"

Networking sounds a lot more formal than it actually is, and it is an invaluable tool in your journey. Simply put, networking is about getting to know people who can help develop your career. Research shows that upwards of 80% of all jobs are found through networking! That's a good enough reason to get started, right?

Think of networking as a conversation to learn about people, professions, and industries rather than an attempt to impress them or land a job. It's a little like dating (without the winking and flirting). Most people are happy to talk about themselves and will be pleased to help, so don't be afraid to ask for advice and information… just don't ask them to help you get a job!

Start with people you know, and keep it informal—meet over coffee. Ask them to suggest a couple more contacts as this is an easy way to start building your network. Once you're more confident, join relevant social media groups and go to professional events.

Get Some Experience

Work experience is just as much about finding your path as it is adding kudos to your CV/resume. In today's competitive environment, it's becoming an essential tool for getting a job. According to the "Graduate Market in 2019" report[19], more than four-fifths of the UK's top graduate employers offered

---

19 High Flyers Research, "The Graduate Market in 2019: Annual Review of Graduate Vacancies & Starting Salaries at The UK's Leading Employers," https://www.highfliers.co.uk/download/2019/graduate_market/GMReport19.pdf

paid work experience programs to students and recent graduates during the 2018-2019 academic year.

If you haven't got any internships or work experience under your belt from your student days, you probably have to knuckle down and live on beans on toast for a few more months while you add more color to your canvas.

Look After Yourself

Your university days are done, so it's time to say no to the 11th pint, say yes to cooking up a feast without pot noodles, and get to bed before 4 am. Start looking after yourself. This may be obvious, but did you know that good physical health can increase your resistance to stress?

Here are a few tips on how to keep yourself healthy:

- **Eat Well**

    Ever heard of the "food-mood" connection? What we eat affects how we feel, and how we feel affects what we choose to eat or drink. A healthy diet benefits mental health, improves energy levels, and keeps you more alert and better able to handle stress. So, don't skip meals, eat your five a day, and drink six to eight glasses a day—of water, that is!

- **Stay Fit**

    Apart from the obvious physical benefits, regular exercise is also known to boost your mood. Exercise pumps up endorphins, triggering a positive feeling which helps you relax and even sleep better. Aim for at least 30 minutes of moderate exercise five times a week. Nothing manic; don't panic! If you don't love sports, go for a bike ride, take the dog for a walk, or tie yourself in yoga knots. Scientists have found that even five minutes of aerobic exercise can stimulate anti-anxiety effects. But hey, you can do better than five!

- **Get Deep Sleep**

    We all know a good night's sleep is important for wellbeing, but just what goes on when you sleep? Your brain recharges, your cells repair themselves, and your body releases important hormones.

And did you know "you'll die from sleep deprivation before food deprivation? It takes two weeks to starve but 10 days without sleep can kill you."[20]

Talk to People

Graduation can be a lonely time. Maybe you've moved to a new area away from university friends and family, or you're under pressure to find a job and think that everyone else has already got their lives together (they haven't!). It can be tempting to shut yourself away if you're not feeling your best. Just know the feeling of "graduation blues" is extremely common, so meet and talk to your friends—they probably feel as you do. Talking through problems can help by giving you a different perspective and helping you find solutions. And besides, enjoying time with friends and family is always a great stress reliever!

A special thank you to Julie and Sophie Phillipson from HelloGrads for sharing these helpful tips with us.

The Journey Ahead

We set out to convince students that LinkedIn is the best tool at their disposal to find a career they love and assure educators that LinkedIn can play an essential part in their curricula. We hope we succeeded in our mission. Far more than this, we hope this book will help students and graduates become confident professionals. For us, it is about making young people feel inspired and excited by their potential and the vast number of career opportunities available to them.

We know we can't cover everything about LinkedIn in one book and much will change about LinkedIn in the coming years. However, we've done our best to focus on strategies that won't change anytime soon, demonstrating the power and benefit of using LinkedIn for your career development. We have laid out these strategies in easy to understand and follow steps. Still,

---

20 The Better Sleep Council, "Geek Out on Sleep with these 16 Surprising Facts," https://bettersleep.org/research/sleep-facts/

we know it's a lot to digest. That's why we encourage you to keep re-reading the book and repeating the steps until you feel comfortable implementing them.

We are confident that if you apply the knowledge you've acquired in this book, you will have a stellar professional brand, the tools to build a great network, and the ability to position yourself as an authority on whichever subject(s) you find most fascinating. This approach will pay dividends throughout your career. More importantly, by staying mentally and physically healthy and diving into a job you love, we hope you can make the life YOU want to live a reality.

If this book has inspired you to see what's possible on LinkedIn, share it with an educator so they can read the last chapter and help set you and other students up for great success using LinkedIn. Thank you for reading! We'd love for you to share your thoughts with us.

CHAPTER 12

LINKEDIN FOR EDUCATORS: PREPARE STUDENTS FOR SUCCESS

To illustrate the value of teaching LinkedIn to students, Melonie shares this story.

"A couple of years ago, I interviewed Rod Ross, a high school teacher from British Columbia, Canada. I had heard that Rod was doing some really great things in an entrepreneurship class for grade 11 students. As part of the curriculum, Rod asked his students to register for LinkedIn. It was this simple action—going directly to the source, the entrepreneurs—that inevitably changed the way his students understood entrepreneurialism. He asked them to develop connections with professionals in their community who were running their businesses or supporting other entrepreneurs.

As part of the experience, Rod also encouraged his students to attend conferences to meet entrepreneurs and then add those contacts to their LinkedIn networks.

One of Rod's students remembers how much this impacted him even though he did not realize it at the time. While he was not using LinkedIn every day as a high school or university student, he started understanding the concept of networking and building up confidence to approach professionals he didn't know.

It also helped that LinkedIn was sending him regular reminders about people requesting to connect with him as well as suggesting with whom he might like to connect next. When Rod's student graduated from high school and arrived at business school, he realized he was far ahead of the LinkedIn curve compared to other students. He already had a well-developed profile and an extensive network, helping him understand the job market and career opportunities across the world.

During the summer, this student traveled to Hong Kong to meet the CEO of a trading company, securing an internship position. Thanks to LinkedIn, he had connected with many leaders and read the latest news from the company. He knew he needed to research the company's employees and follow their company page to get a sense of what they did so he could answer interview questions more effectively. Because he took the time to connect with a variety of employees and understand the latest developments at the company, he was better prepared for the hiring process than most candidates, landing the internship he was after."

It is amazing that a high school teacher had the wisdom and foresight to get his students using LinkedIn so early in their education. He understood that to promote the right mindset and behaviors in his students, he needed to teach them a mix of soft skills and digital awareness.

This is the outcome we want educators to achieve with their students when using LinkedIn. We want them to see it as not only another social media channel or online tool but also a conduit to support useful professional behaviors. That's because such behaviors lead to more advanced career developments, and promoting such behaviors can fit nicely in any curriculum.

Where do you start?

This is the first piece of advice we offer to educators: Once your students register for your class, connect with them on LinkedIn. If you are not comfortable doing it, you are not alone. Many educators don't feel comfortable doing it because of their perception of the way other social media platforms are being used. You might think connecting with students is inappropriate, or you don't see the value of doing it. It's okay to feel that way about Facebook, but nothing is further from the truth when it comes to LinkedIn.

LinkedIn is *not* Facebook or Instagram. You are not connecting to be friends with your students and share selfies with them. You are connecting with your students because that is what professionals do every day. We used to exchange business cards and add contacts to our Rolodex; today, we exchange LinkedIn profiles and add connections to our online networks. Your students can benefit significantly from getting on LinkedIn early and using you as a connection to many other people and opportunities.

Here are eight great reasons to connect and support your students on LinkedIn:

1. You can encourage your students to learn more about you, which can help you build stronger, more meaningful professional relationships with them.

2. You can help raise their interest in a particular subject by showing them how different theories and concepts are applied in the real world.

3. You can introduce them to other academics and professionals who can provide further guidance on what courses to take or careers to consider.

4. You can use LinkedIn as a way to share exciting or valuable updates on current events applicable to what you are teaching.

5. You can demonstrate opportunities available to your students after graduation and how to prepare for them.

6. You can include LinkedIn in your lesson plans and assignments to help students find ways to build their professional brands outside the classroom.

7. You can use LinkedIn to communicate with your students using a group or LinkedIn's messenger. This includes sharing links and useful content that enhance your curriculum before, during, and after each lesson.

8. You can help your students find internships and other work experience opportunities aligned with what they're learning while still at school.

Making LinkedIn a Part of Student Learning

One of the objectives of this chapter is to help universities and other educational institutions understand the value of making LinkedIn an essential part of every curriculum and learning program. LinkedIn education should no longer be something that career services take care of through short sessions or something that is promoted a few times a year to small groups of students. If LinkedIn is misunderstood and not used by the school's staff and faculty, it's highly likely that students will fail to see its value as well.

The other thing to realize is LinkedIn is not just a profile and place for students to copy and paste their resumes/CVs. This is by far the single biggest mistake and misconception educators make about LinkedIn. Much focus is placed on the LinkedIn profile, and the advice is so simplistic that students see it as a box-checking exercise on a long to-do list of university tasks. Such limited approach does not benefit them.

No wonder so many students rarely, if ever, visit their LinkedIn profiles during their student years. They consider registering and having a profile to be the end of the journey with LinkedIn while they are students. They think all the other stuff they see isn't for them—it's for people with more experience. We know this because when we ask students about LinkedIn, they typically tell us they plan to use it closer to graduation or after they graduate and start looking for jobs.

Unfortunately, leaving it until the end of their student journey means they will have a long, steep learning curve. By the time they graduate, they need to have extensive professional networks to aid their careers. Instead, they will be starting from zero. This can be during a stressful time when they are trying to find what's next in their lives after university, which makes it even harder for them to use LinkedIn effectively for their career development.

Many of the essential soft skills students need to succeed in today's workplace can be practiced through the use of LinkedIn. These include self-awareness, self-development, communication, networking, business writing, presentation, and emotional intelligence. Students can start discovering their strengths, weaknesses, and personal preferences that may or may not be well suited for their chosen career paths. They can start learning about the requirements and qualifications they need to have to be considered for specific roles.

As they get in touch with other professionals, they will get exposure to different communication styles, helping them adapt their approaches. With time, your students will have the potential of building valuable relationships with hundreds of employers on LinkedIn. They will get used to the idea of connecting and writing messages to people they don't know so that they can find new avenues to career opportunities. When the time comes to sit down in front of these employers, your students will already be the type of professionals who can present the best they have to offer because they understand who they are and whom they want to become.

To make LinkedIn a part of student learning, you first need to understand the needs and ambitions of your students. If you cannot connect with them on a personal level, it's unlikely you'll be able to offer them something that truly makes a difference. You want to make sure that before encouraging students to create or complete their LinkedIn profiles, you first learn about their professional interests and potential career paths they would like to explore.

You could send out surveys or questionnaires to scale this approach and then group students into different categories, depending on their interests. This would allow you to give targeted advice about LinkedIn aligned with the interests of each student. It could be based on specific industries, organizations, departments, roles, or even the type of products and services offered by different companies.

Here are some LinkedIn activities you could recommend to your students:

1. Research the company page of different organizations to learn more about what they do, the type of workplace they offer, and the current roles available there.
2. Use specific search criteria to discover people and companies related to their professional interests and career goals.

3. Connect with staff and faculty who can help them (a) decide the best action plan to follow and (b) find people with whom to speak to get career advice and support.

4. Connect with any employers from the community who can offer them advice and work experience opportunities.

5. Read specific articles and posts from influencers and industry leaders that reveal the current thinking and future priorities of businesses.

6. Turn essays or similar assignments into published articles on LinkedIn that can showcase their strengths and build up their professional brands.

7. Choose people and companies to follow that will help them keep in touch with potential future employers and stay in the know about what's happening in the industry.

Especially in the beginning, it's important to know your students and give them as much guidance as possible on the use of LinkedIn. Don't expect them to have a complete profile on day one. Instead, give them enough time to explore LinkedIn to discover what resonates with them most. They need to be able to see LinkedIn for what it is—a highly useful networking tool that can supercharge their learning and professional development. To see this, they need to find the kinds of topics, people, and organizations that reflect their values, interests, and ambitions. Simply put, they need to feel inspired by how LinkedIn can change their lives and careers.

Inspiring Your Students

In our workshops, we show videos of how other people have used LinkedIn to define and pursue their versions of success. Usually, participants are quite surprised by these videos because they show ordinary people using LinkedIn in creative and extraordinary ways that exceed their expectations.

Unless students feel inspired and excited about the opportunities LinkedIn can give them, it's nearly impossible to motivate them to use it. If they don't clearly understand what's in it for them, they won't accomplish much and will be discouraged to use it further.

We hope you can see now why you'd want your students to develop genuine interest in LinkedIn. Profile creation or professional branding workshops are not likely to get them excited. Many students see such sessions as extra work they need to think about and do. It's disappointing to hear they don't have time to dedicate to LinkedIn. It's even more disappointing to hear they don't feel they have enough support to learn to use it correctly, yet their sentiment is understandable.

Despite the fact that today's students have grown up with technology and social media, they don't know how to use LinkedIn. After all, it is not a site where they message their friends or post photos from their travels, so they usually feel very uncomfortable using it. Without proper direction and understanding of the tremendous value it can bring them in landing their dream jobs and sustaining successful careers, they will flounder.

LinkedIn can no longer be an afterthought for students and professionals. At the same time, students need to become self-driven enough to learn how to use LinkedIn effectively. To inspire your students to use LinkedIn like professionals, you need to design and run useful and meaningful LinkedIn training sessions for them.

To help you develop relevant LinkedIn curriculum, ask recruiters and hiring managers the following questions:

- How do they use LinkedIn to find and get in touch with candidates?
- What are the top things they are looking for?
- What annoys them the most, and what do they consider unacceptable on LinkedIn?
- What's the best way for students and graduates to get in touch with them when inquiring about jobs?

Invite successful alumni as well as other experts and leaders in their fields to describe how they use LinkedIn. Collect these examples so you can share them with your students, whether it's through newsletters, lectures, online learning portals, or one-on-one sessions.

Look closely at the career trajectories of these different professionals so you can illustrate the variety of different ways students can approach their own job search and career development. It is very encouraging for students to see that a linear path toward career success is rare. What better way to prove this notion than by letting professionals share their experiences with the students?

Finally, ask your colleagues to recognize all the great work their students do by (a) endorsing them for specific skills and (b) writing them recommendations on LinkedIn. These testimonials of their skills and abilities will appear on their profiles and will be extremely valuable when recruiters and hiring managers consider the students for potential positions.

Project Plans for Students

We firmly believe that LinkedIn can be a robust research and collaboration tool for student projects. Just think of the immense value students would get from interacting with leaders and experts in their networks to gather additional data and insights—information that wouldn't be available anywhere else. LinkedIn would help students not only complete their coursework in new and exciting ways but also build essential relationships with employers.

In the past few years, we have worked with some of the leading universities in the UK promoting student research opportunities. Within these research modules, groups of students partner with many different organizations to help them solve a particular challenge or develop new products and services.

These programs usually last about ten weeks, and students partner with different stakeholders in the organization, who provide advice and guidance throughout the process. At the end of the project, students present their findings and solutions. This could be a presentation, business plan, or a prototype of an idea.

We worked with several of these universities to help them understand how LinkedIn could help facilitate the communication and collaboration among the student teams, program sponsors, and partner organizations.

LinkedIn was a great way for students to promote their projects and provide regular updates on their progress. This, in turn, provided them with great comments and feedback from their networks. Students received not only input from their peers and faculty but also valuable feedback from professionals in the industry, who had a good understanding of the challenges and opportunities the students faced with their projects. You can imagine how excited the students were to get recognition and validation for their work from experts from around the world!

While we understand why certain assignments and projects might not translate well into LinkedIn, we don't see why most of the work a student does at a university could not benefit from their use of LinkedIn. At a minimum, educators should be encouraging students to share the work and achievements they are most proud of with their LinkedIn networks. This is not about boasting; rather, it is about promoting their passions and showcasing their abilities. Your students have an opportunity to let employers know they are not just students—they are young and ambitious professionals preparing for the future.

As more universities search for ways to make career development part of their curricula, we believe LinkedIn can play a significant role in this strategy. More than ever, students need to be exposed to the world of work earlier in their journeys. So much is changing so quickly, and to adapt to this frantic pace, students will have to join the race or risk being left behind before they even have a chance to reach the starting line. Be the kind of educator who helps students become successful professionals.

Professional Brand Assessment

The professional brand of a student must answer one simple question: *What's unique about my experience?* More than anything else, employers want to have the answer to this question from a graduate who may not have as much work experience as other professionals. This is why it's imperative you help students build a professional brand showcasing the best of who they are and whom they want to become. To accomplish that, focus on their character, variety and quality of their experiences, and achieved results.

Here's a checklist that can help you design a professional brand assessment for your students:

- ☐ My photo, headline, and About section represent the best of what I have to offer.

- ☐ I have included media such as images, videos, and presentations to highlight my work.
- ☐ My Experience section includes my title, name of the organization, and my accomplishments during each job.
- ☐ To highlight all my experience, I have added my projects, volunteering, and extra-curricular work.
- ☐ I have asked for recommendations from people who have worked with me and can vouch for my skills.
- ☐ My Education section promotes what I have learned and achieved beyond my student life.
- ☐ I have shared my knowledge by publishing articles showcasing my interests and ideas.

Consider setting up a photo session for students to take professional headshots. It is crucial students take this seriously and understand that they should look in the photo the way they'd want to look at an interview.

Make sure the headlines under their names on their profiles don't just say they are students or graduates. Ask them to highlight what they are really good at in a few words or write a short statement that includes keywords recruiters in the industry use to search for candidates.

Help them write an About section that reflects their personality and tells a unique story demonstrating the type of professional they are.

Another important thing to include on the profile is content representing their portfolio, with clear examples of any work the student has done that can be shared publicly. You can include media in this part of the profile, bringing to life the work of students to make up for the lack of work experience. Employers will at least get an opportunity to see the skill level and evidence of the work the student can produce.

Beyond adding media to their profiles, such as images and videos, encourage your students to provide descriptions of what the content represents and the role they played in creating it if applicable. It's even better to encourage students to publish updates or articles about their work as these will also appear on their profiles under their Activity sections.

Network and Outreach Assessment

The network and outreach assessments measure:

a. the quantity and quality of your students' LinkedIn connections

b. the level of engagement of your students with their networks.

The metrics include likes, comments, shares, connection requests, and messages.

It is important students build up a good number of connections on LinkedIn. Typically, students have a very low number of connections throughout their time at university—below 100. Since much of the value of using LinkedIn is derived from the relationships your students can build with other professionals, the low number of connections significantly diminishes their opportunities to make the most of LinkedIn.

Encourage students to make at least 200, preferably 500, connections within the regions, industries, and organizations they care about. It will be more difficult for them to be discovered by recruiters and hiring managers if they have only a few connections.

Here's a checklist that can help you design a network and outreach assessment for your students:

- ☐ I am connecting with people at the companies and industries that interest me.
- ☐ I am messaging my connections to learn more about what they do and what they enjoy about their work.
- ☐ I am scheduling calls and meetings to help me build valuable relationships that can lead to career opportunities.
- ☐ I am attending events, webinars, and meetups that can further expand my network and develop my industry knowledge, then connecting with the people I meet in person on LinkedIn.
- ☐ I am consistently asking for help in a professional manner and offering value to my network.
- ☐ I am using LinkedIn's advanced search functionality to find better quality results.

☐ I am searching using all filters for people, jobs, content, companies, groups, and schools.

☐ I have created job alerts so I can receive emails and mobile notifications about the roles I am interested in.

☐ I have researched people who have the positions I am looking for so I can understand what I need to focus on.

☐ I am examining company pages to find out what they do and the type of workplace culture they have.

☐ I can describe the responsibilities and requirements of the jobs that interest me.

☐ I am paying attention to the language used in job descriptions to make sure I include similar language within my profile and in the messages I send.

This assessment should challenge students to think and act carefully when building their networks, searching for opportunities, and applying for jobs on LinkedIn. They will learn more about themselves and what it means to find the right fit by making sure that what they are looking for is aligned with who they are and what they would enjoy doing. In addition, they will build a network of allies that can help them succeed throughout each step in their journeys.

Career Planning Assessment

The career planning assessment is the ultimate guide to help students transform into professionals as they forge their paths toward their careers. Now, it is all about taking actions and creating opportunities by attracting and connecting with the right people.

Here's a checklist that can help you design a career planning assessment for your students:

☐ I am making it obvious that I am looking for specific opportunities where I am confident I am the right fit.

- ☐ I am asking my allies to refer me for particular job opportunities to speed up the recruitment process.

- ☐ I am reaching out to employees in the companies I am interested in working at who can reveal more about the job being offered.

- ☐ I am going above and beyond the application process to get noticed by recruiters and hiring managers by proactively connecting and reaching out to them to ask for more information.

- ☐ I am sharing my insights and posting interesting content on LinkedIn relevant to the position I have applied for, the value the organization offers to their customers, and the problems it helps solve so I can stay top of mind.

- ☐ I am creating my own content and writing articles showcasing my interests, knowledge, and enthusiasm, bringing to life who I am and my long-term career potential.

We are confident students taking all these steps will be approached by more recruiters, will be able to secure more interviews, and will eventually get better jobs. Don't worry if it takes students longer to get to this point and pass this assessment. This usually pushes them way beyond their comfort zones.

As an educator, you can help students by doing some background work yourself. Perhaps you can reach out to employers and find out more about their hiring processes. You can offer to review anything students plan to share on LinkedIn, whether it's a short update or long article, and give them feedback before they post it. Finally, you can research specific jobs related to student interests and guide them towards applying. Just make sure you make them do the heavy lifting.

CONCLUSION

We are tired of seeing many students and graduates fail to get the jobs they want, falling into uninspiring roles harmful to their health and wellbeing. Much of this could be avoided if we teach students to use LinkedIn throughout their student journeys to discover and rediscover who they are and what they can do to get better.

We hope that as educators, no matter what you do inside or outside the classroom or lecture hall, you'll use LinkedIn to level the playing field for your students. Send them that initial connection request on LinkedIn, and give every single one of them the chance to redefine and surpass their career standards and expectations. With your guidance, we know LinkedIn can make a real difference in their lives, and in the process, you will build a lasting legacy you can be proud of.

With over half a billion of the world's professionals on LinkedIn today, there will never be a shortage of amazing people with amazing stories to inspire us to achieve more. Somewhere in there, your students will find what they have always been looking for but couldn't quite describe.

…

If this book has inspired you to see what's possible on LinkedIn, please suggest it to someone who would also benefit from it.

Melonie & Miguel

ABOUT THE AUTHORS

Melonie Dodaro is a preeminent authority on LinkedIn and social selling, author of multiple #1 bestselling books, including *LinkedIn Unlocked*, and creator of numerous online training and coaching programs.

She helps individuals, businesses, governments, and universities tap into and maximize the possibilities of LinkedIn for lead generation, marketing and career development.

Global ranking and industry recognition (partial list):

- Top 100 Digital Marketers (by Brand24)
- Top 50 Sales Influencers (by Onalytica)
- Top 10 Social Media Blogs (by Social Media Examiner)
- Top 100 Marketing Influencers (by Tenfold)
- 10 Social Influencers on LinkedIn: Social Selling Leaders to Follow (by Wiley)

In addition to using her books as teaching tools, she teaches her proprietary methods through online programs, workshops, and training seminars and is a contributing author at *Social Media Examiner*, *LinkedIn Sales Solutions Blog*, *LinkedIn Marketing Solutions Blog*, *Canadian Business Journal*, and has been featured in *Forbes*, *Entrepreneur*, *Inc.*, and numerous other publications.

Email Melonie at: info@topdogsocialmedia.com

Miguel Ángel Garcia Elizondo is a passionate advocate for improving education and career development opportunities for young people. Miguel has helped hundreds of disadvantaged high school students to apply successfully to a number of different universities across Texas since 2006.

His passion to use education and technology to change the way people live and work led him to London in 2010, where he had the opportunity to work for companies such as Microsoft, LinkedIn, and Sprinklr. Since then, he's helped thousands of students and graduates to learn new skills and find professional opportunities that have improved their lives.

Today, Miguel continues mentoring students and professionals, and has recently worked with local government to offer enhanced career services to staff and residents.

Email Miguel at: miguel@fylolearning.com

REFERENCES

Bate, Nicholas. *Do What You Want: The Book that Shows You How to Create a Career You'll Love.* Toronto: Pearson Education Canada, 2012.

Bell, Elliott. "How a Simple LinkedIn Message That Took 2 Minutes to Write Landed Me My Dream Job." *The Muse.* https://www.themuse.com/advice/how-a-simple-linkedin-message-that-took-2-minutes-to-write-landed-me-my-dream-job

Carroll, Katie. "Top Companies 2019: Where the UK Wants to Work Now." *LinkedIn.* April 2, 2019. https://www.linkedin.com/pulse/top-companies-2019-where-uk-wants-work-now-katie-carroll

High Flyers Research. "The Graduate Market in 2019: Annual Review of Graduate Vacancies & Starting Salaries at The UK's Leading Employers." https://www.highfliers.co.uk/download/2019/graduate_market/GMReport19.pdf

Hoffman, Reid. *The Start-Up of You: Adapt to the Future, Invest in Yourself and Transform Your Career.* New York: Currency, 2012.

Hoffman, Reid, Ben Casnocha, and Chris Yeh. *The Alliance: Managing Talent in the Networked Age.* Boston: Harvard Business Review Press, 2014.

Jessen, Catherine. "10 Shocking Stats About Employee Engagement." *The Muse.* https://www.themuse.com/advice/10-shocking-stats-about-employee-engagement

Kotler, Steven. "The Passion Recipe: Four Steps to Total Fulfilment." *Forbes.* March 27, 2015. https://www.forbes.com/sites/stevenkotler/2015/03/27/the-passion-recipe-four-steps-to-total-fulfillment

Lewis, Gregory. "The Most In-Demand Hard Skills and Soft Skills of 2019." *LinkedIn*. January 3, 2019. https://business.linkedin.com/talent-solutions/blog/trends-and-research/2018/the-most-in-demand-hard-and-soft-skills-of-2018

LinkedIn. "LinkedIn 2018 Emerging Jobs Report." December 13, 2018. https://economicgraph.linkedin.com/research/linkedin-2018-emerging-jobs-report

Marchal, Jenny. "How to Find Your Ideal Career Path Without Wasting Time on Jobs Not Suitable for You." *Lifehack*. https://www.lifehack.org/585462/how-decide-career

Pendell, Ryan, and Jim Harter. "10 Gallup Reports to Share with Your Leaders in 2019." *Gallup*. January 4, 2019. https://www.gallup.com/workplace/245786/gallup-reports-share-leaders-2019.aspx

PricewaterhouseCoopers. "Workforce of the Future: The Competing Forces Shaping 2030." https://www.pwc.com/gx/en/services/people-organisation/publications/workforce-of-the-future.html

Roth, Daniel. "Top Companies 2019: Where the U.S. Wants to Work Now." *LinkedIn*. https://www.linkedin.com/pulse/top-companies-2019-where-us-wants-work-now-daniel-roth

Rowan, Sophie. *Brilliant Career Coach: How to Find and Follow Your Dream Career*. Harlow: Pearson Education Limited, 2011.

Serwer, Andy. "Warren Buffett Shares His Keys to Success." *Yahoo Finance* video. 2:32. April 18, 2019. https://news.yahoo.com/warren-buffett-shares-keys-success-134329028.html

Silva, Jason. "How to Find Your Passion." *YouTube* video. 2:11. June 7, 2016. https://www.youtube.com/watch?v=HScOL_aOMrw

The Better Sleep Council. "Geek Out on Sleep with these 16 Surprising Facts." https://bettersleep.org/research/sleep-facts/

Trought, Frances. *Brilliant Employability Skills: How to Stand Out from the Crowd in the Graduate Job Market*. Harlow: Pearson Education Limited, 2012.